THE BIG BOOK OF
CRYPTID
TRIVIA

**Fun Facts and Fascinating Folklore about
Bigfoot, Mothman, Loch Ness Monster, the
Yeti, and More Elusive Creatures**

BERNADETTE JOHNSON

Published by:
Ulysses Press
PO Box 3440
Berkeley, CA 94703
www.ulyssespress.com

ISBN: 978-1-64604-494-8
Library of Congress Control Number: 2023930702

Printed in the United States by Kingery Printing Company
10 9 8 7 6 5 4 3 2 1

Acquisitions editor: Casie Vogel
Managing editor: Claire Chun
Project editor: Paulina Maurovich
Editor: Scott Calamar
Proofreader: Renee Rutledge
Front cover design: Elke Barter
Interior design and layout: Winnie Liu
Cover artwork: Bigfoot © Athenaeum creations/shutterstock.com; frame and leather background © RK1919/envato.com

To Jeff and our furry little monster, Molly.

CONTENTS

FOREWORD

THE CRYPTOZOOLOGY CHALLENGE

You might be surprised to find a book of trivia on cryptozo-ology. You might even say that cryptozoology, in general, is a trivial pursuit. However, the origins of trivia are intriguing in the context of the word "trivia."

The ancient Romans used the word *triviae* to describe where one road split or forked into two roads. Triviae was formed from *tri* (three) and *viae* (roads)—literally meaning "three roads." It was introduced into English as the adjective "trivial" in the fifteenth and sixteenth centuries.

Traditionally, trivia is used to convey nuggets of information in academic settings, barroom games, and challenges (question-and-answer sessions) among students. Trivia is also discussed on camping trips by Bigfoot hunters. "Regular" or "basic" educational ventures revolve around grammar, logic, and rhetoric versus higher education that involve music, astronomy, geometry, and mathematics.

The term issues from the Greek and Latin meanings regarding choosing your way down one of three paths. The major three routes for cryptozoology are:

1. Investigations of the cryptids for evidence that some are new species

2. Skepticism of the nature of some reported cryptids even existing, and

3. Realization that a few certain cryptids may be a hoax

After interacting for over six decades in the field of cryptozoology, I've seen a great deal of historical changes and word evolutions. Since I've investigated many cryptids and shared the cases for which I have been the primary researcher, I've often invented names for certain creatures encountered and examined. The names Dover Demon, Montauk Monster, Phantom Panthers, Winged Weirdies, and Leeds Loki are cryptids I coined that reflect my love of alliteration. Other creatures I've named, such as Cassie, the Casco Bay Sea Serpent, follow in the tradition of Nessie, Bessie, and Wessie. Still others I've named, like Napes, for the Northern American Apes, and the Marked Hominids, inspired by cryptozoologist Mark A. Hall, come about through direct connections.

Additionally, trivia has been expanded by the naming of cryptid-inhabited locations, such as the Bridgewater Triangle in Massachusetts and the Aroostook Triangle in Maine, which I personally coined.

My in-depth research on cryptid events that have resulted in file cabinets full of sightings of alligators-in-the-sewers and out-of-place crocs, as well as Phantom Kangaroos seen throughout North America (where they shouldn't be), confounds trivia buffs daily.

What happens with all these monikers, names, and terms is intriguing. For example, in the beginning of the history of Bigfoot studies in 1958, zoologist and cryptozoologist Ivan T. Sanderson was not a fan of the use of the name Bigfoot. He understood that the precursor term Sasquatch was not going to work because it was, after all, regionally based and very

Canadian. Sanderson thought the better candidate would be Oh-Mah, a Hoopa word for Bigfoot. Sanderson wanted Oh-Mah to catch on, but it never did. Sasquatch has not been used interchangeably either, and Bigfoot has spread around the world to replace Yeren, Yowie, Yeti, Snowman, and every local name for unknown hairy hominids, especially by the media.

Sanderson's first use of "cryptozoological" did not appear until 1961, in his book *Abominable Snowmen: Legend Come to Life* (Philadelphia: Chilton). Words take time to leak into the culture.

Thus, I was surprised when forty years after I coined the name Dover Demon, I discovered that action figure replicas were being made in Japan. I had little realized the phrase had become that famous.

The term "cryptozoology" (from the Greek) perfectly fits the idea of hidden (*kryptos*) animal (*zoon*) study (*logos*). Worthy of noting is that before its widespread employment, the word "cryptozoology" developed between the 1920s and 1940s. The early concept was expressed through the phrase "romantic zoology."

Willy Ley's *The Lungfish and the Unicorn* (1941) was revised and retitled as *The Lungfish, the Dodo, and the Unicorn* (1948). Both shared the subtitle "An Excursion into Romantic Zoology." Romantic zoology grew out of the Victorian era of exploration and initial contact with indigenous peoples. Western and Eastern science was interested in categorizing the entire natural world and identifying new animals through observations, folklore, and capture.

Cryptozoology extended these methods to discover and verify new species. But romantic zoologists were well aware that local native peoples were there first. Indeed, collectors of new species for museums and zoos knew the best sources of information were the indigenous people who already had names and recognized their local wildlife. I know this from history and my Cherokee ancestors. Many people in the twenty-first century learn the information through trivia.

The idea that Columbus discovered America is as nonsensical as saying the Germans, Belgians, and British first discovered the Okapi in the Congo. Everyone knew the Efe African Pygmies of the Ituri Rainforest were there first. So those were the people the Westerners interviewed. A mere three decades later, the coelacanth, which had been eaten by locals for centuries, was "discovered" to be a "living fossil" by a woman museum director in South Africa.

Two success stories in cryptozoology: Tales of a striped donkey in the jungles of Africa turned out to be true in 1901, and a bad-tasting fish known from the time of the dinosaurs was revealed in 1938.

Enjoy this book and learn new tidbits of the adventure.

Loren Coleman, Director
International Cryptozoology Museum
March 13, 2023

***

Loren Coleman has been involved in cryptozoology since March 1960 and has investigated cases from North America to Loch Ness. He has degrees in anthropology, zoology, and psychiatric social work; has written over forty books; and produced and/or appeared in over forty movies, reality programs, and documentaries. He is the director and founder of the nonprofit International Cryptozoology Museum. Coleman's books include *Mysterious America*; *Cryptozoology A to Z*; and *Bigfoot: True Story of Apes in America*.

INTRODUCTION

We've all likely heard wild tales of creatures that we assume are either myths or hoaxes but in which some people fervently believe. The most famous are arguably Bigfoot (aka Sasquatch) and the Loch Ness Monster (aka Nessie). These creatures are called "cryptids": animals that some think exist but for which there is no solid scientific evidence. The study of these possibly mythical, folkloric creatures is called "cryptozoology," and the people who embark on this study are called "cryptozoologists."

Cryptozoology is considered by many to be a pseudoscience, but historically there has been some overlap between naturalists, zoologists, and other credentialed scientists and the study of cryptids, especially back in the days when the population was smaller, world travel was difficult, and many animals known in some parts of the world were unknown—or known only through fanciful tales—in others.

Cryptids range from the aforementioned Nessie and Sasquatch to hyperlocal creatures of legend, and they run the gamut in geographical location, size, description, and biological class. From worms to fish to fowl to reptiles to big cats to hairy hominids, some are fanciful, like giant sea serpents or fearsome blood-sucking monsters with hooves and wings and claws and glowing red eyes, but others have descriptions that could plausibly be of creatures that have remained hidden somewhere deep in the forests or oceans or high in the mountains. And some are even animals that did exist but are now believed extinct by all but a few true believers. Even germs were considered cryptids at one point. Who would have believed the first person who said that tiny living creatures that were too small for us to see were making people sick?

In this book, you will read about dozens of cryptids spoken of, and sometimes reportedly seen, all over the world, like a deadly poison-spitting worm in the Gobi Desert, aquatic lake dwellers in Tahoe and the Congo basin, a bat-like creature in Java, several half-man, half-animal hybrids in the US, and lots of ape-men from the Americas to the Himalayas to the mountains of Japan.

Some cryptids were appropriated and metamorphosed from the legends of Indigenous peoples, and others resulted and spread from reported sightings.

You will also learn about eye-witness testimonies and (mostly blurry) photographs that some consider proof, as well as possible alternative scientific explanations put forth for some of the sightings. Indeed, some animals were once considered mythical before they were found and identified by scientists in real life. You'll be surprised to find out how recently the western world "discovered" the existence of gorillas!

It isn't unreasonable to study cryptids, and the belief in cryptids, and to come at such study with a healthy mix of skepticism and open-mindedness. Plus they're fun! Who wouldn't be delighted to discover dinosaurs that escaped the notice of scientists until now? Or to find out dragons or unicorns were real?

In this volume, uncover the mysteries of fantastic beasts, real and imagined, and where at least some people think they can be found. Also, dig into local lore surrounding cryptids, cryptid tourism, cryptids in pop culture, notable hoaxes, and real animal discoveries. Whether you are a seasoned skeptic, a budding cryptozoologist, or something in between, this book is sure to include facts and oddities that intrigue, educate, and entertain.

Happy reading!

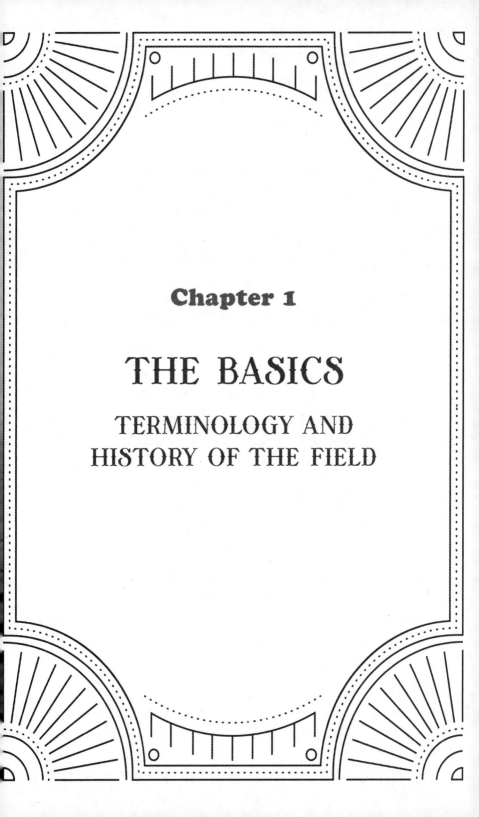

Chapter 1

THE BASICS

TERMINOLOGY AND HISTORY OF THE FIELD

Q: What is cryptozoology?

A: Cryptozoology is the study of cryptids, which are creatures that are considered mythological by most people, but that some people believe exist. For instance, Bigfoot and the Loch Ness Monster are two such cryptids for which there are a great many skeptics, including most zoologists, but some die-hard believers. The word "cryptozoology" is widely thought to have been coined by Belgian-French zoologist Bernard Heuvelmans in the 1950s, but Heuvelmans himself credited British biologist Ivan T. Sanderson with coining the word in the 1940s.

Q: What are people who study cryptids called?

A: As you would expect, someone who studies cryptozoology is a cryptozoologist.

Q: When was the term "cryptid" coined?

A: Although "cryptozoology" was coined in the 1950s, and the word "cryptid" was derived from "cryptozoology," the first usage of "cryptid" was in a letter to the editor written by John E. Wall published in a 1983 edition of the *International Society of Cryptozoology (ISC) Newsletter*.

Q: What is the etymology of the word "cryptozoology"?

A: The word "cryptozoology" is a melding of the Greek word *kryptos*, meaning hidden, with the word "zoology," the scientific study of animals. "Zoology" comes from the Greek words *zoion* (meaning animal) and *logia* (meaning study).

Q: What is a hominid?

A: Cryptids like Bigfoot and the Yeti are often referred to as hominids. In biological taxonomy, a hominid is a member of the family Hominidae, which includes bipedal primates who stand (or stood) erect, including modern humans, some of our extinct ancestors, extinct relatives like the Neanderthals, and in some modern classifications, also the great apes, including the bonobo, chimpanzee, gorilla, and orangutan.

Q: What is a "globster?"

A: Cryptozoologist Ivan T. Sanderson coined the term "globster" (a portmanteau of "glob" and "monster," perhaps with "lobster" in mind) to describe masses of mangled flesh and bone that occasionally wash up onto beaches and temporarily defy identification, leading to some reports that they are sea serpent carcasses. The first glob of initially unidentified animal that Sanderson dubbed a globster washed ashore in Western Tasmania in 1960 and turned out to be a partial whale carcass.

Q: What is cryptobotany?

A: Whereas the subjects of the study of cryptozoology are animals, cryptobotany is the study of plants that are believed to exist by some but that are not confirmed by science.

Chapter 2

GETTING HAIRY

BIGFOOT, THE YETI, AND OTHER FURRY HOMINIDS

Q: What famous hairy cryptid reportedly calls the Pacific Northwestern region of North America home?

A: Bigfoot, also often called Sasquatch, which is the Canadian version and which predates Bigfoot (see next entry), is arguably the most famous cryptid in the United States. There are innumerable stories about the creature, and he or she appears as a pop culture reference in a great many movies, shows, and commercials, and all over various merchandise. You can even partake in Bigfoot hunting tours. Although there are Bigfoot-type creatures reported all over North America (and similar cryptids the world over), Bigfoot and Sasquatch proper are said to mainly inhabit the forests of the Pacific Northwest region of North America, and are usually described as tall, large, hairy, bipedal humanlike creatures, sometimes completely hair covered and animalistic, and sometimes more like a hairy caveman. As happens with all cryptids, some people fervently believe the creatures exists, but there is as yet no conclusive scientific evidence.

Q: What is the origin of the word Sasquatch?

A: Although Sasquatch is often used interchangeably with Bigfoot these days (and sometimes even with its Himalayan compatriot the Yeti), stories of the Sasquatch predate Bigfoot's 1950s debut by rather a long time, although both refer to hairy hominids who live in the woods of the Pacific Northwest in Canada and the United States. The word Sasquatch was reportedly created in the 1920s by John W. Burns, a Canadian government-appointed teacher on a Sts'ailes (aka Chehalis) reservation in the British Columbia area who gathered stories about the creature from the Indigenous locals (stories that go back hundreds, possibly thousands, of years). He wrote the article "Introducing BC's Hairy Giants," published in *Maclean's* magazine in 1929. The word was apparently a combination and anglicization of several Indigenous groups' names for the beasts—including "sasq'ets," meaning "hairy man" in one of the dialects of the Sts'ailes First Nations people—into a new word.

Q: What publicity stunt propelled Sasquatch to global fame?

A: In 1957, the British Columbia government offered grants for local projects to celebrate their centennial. The resort town of Harrison Hot Springs proposed a Sasquatch hunt. Although the proposal was not approved for the funding, the story reached far and wide, boosting tourism to the area and putting the name Sasquatch into the worldwide public lexicon.

Q: What First Nation tribe of the Pacific Northwest has Sasquatch on their flag?

A: The Sts'ailes First Nations people have inhabited the Harrison River Valley in British Columbia, Canada, for at least ten millennia. They consider Sasquatch a protector of the land, and their flag includes an artistic rendering of the creature. They have also held an annual festival called Sasquatch Days since 1938 that includes people dressed in Sasquatch costume.

Q: When did the name Bigfoot first enter the public lexicon?

A: The term Bigfoot became widespread after an article appeared in a Northern California newspaper, the *Humboldt Times*, on October 5, 1958, written by Andrew Genzoli. The article was prompted by Jerry Crew, a construction worker who had made several plaster casts of large footprints he had found in the Bluff Creek Valley area, one of which he brought to the newspaper office. He and the other construction workers were calling the mysterious creator of these footprints "Bigfoot." Genzoli wrote the name into the article, and the rest is history.

Q: What filmed evidence convinced many of Bigfoot's existence?

A: On October 20, 1967, footage emerged of the elusive Bigfoot, shot in the Bluff Creek area where the famous footprints were discovered and first revealed to the world in 1958. It was a 16 mm film of a tall, female, hairy hominid walking in the woods and was just a few seconds long. The film was made by Bob Gimlin and Roger Patterson, and whether the footage is real or a hoax has been hotly debated, but not yet proven one way or the other.

Q: What cryptid are Sasquatches said to have fought off to protect people?

A: First reportedly encountered by two lumber workers in Wexford County, Michigan, in 1887, the Dogman is a beast that is described as standing about seven feet tall; walking upright like a man; covered in hair, with a head somewhere between that of a wolf and a dog; ears that point upward; sharp fangs; long arms with long, sharp claws; and eyes of either amber, orange, or red that are sometimes described as glowing. There have been a number of reports of Dogman encounters since then, one in which a girl was said to be trapped between two Dogmen who seemed to be communicating with each other (but they eventually left her alone). Some eyewitnesses even claimed that a Sasquatch showed up and protected them by fighting the Dogmen off!

Q: What ability is the Sasquatch known for in Sts'ailes lore?

A: Although often described as a hairy hominid, in Sts'ailes lore, the creature is a shapeshifter who can change into various animals, trees, rocks, and other things that make them harder to find.

Q: What cryptid is said to stalk the Himalayas?

A: The Yeti is a world-famous, large, hairy, bipedal, apelike creature (akin to North America's Bigfoot or Sasquatch) that is said to inhabit the cold, snowy Himalayan mountains in Nepal, Tibet, and Sikkim. Footprint sightings have also been reported in the valleys of the area. Sometimes the Yeti is described as having backward feet.

Q: What is a major physical difference between the Yeti as described in reported sightings versus how it appears in most pop culture depictions?

A: Most pop culture depictions of the Yeti, often also called the Abominable Snowman, are of a fearsome bipedal creature covered in white fur. But in the early accounts from explorers of the region and from the lore of the area, the Yeti is a dark-haired creature.

Q: What is the origin of the name Yeti?

A: One of the names used by the Sherpa people (an ethnic group in the northeast of Nepal and western Tibet in the Himalayas) for the creature we call the Yeti is *Yeh-Teh*, which means "animal of rocky places." Yeti is simply an anglicized mispronunciation of *Yeh-Teh*. Although it may have also derived from *Meh-Teh*, meaning "man-bear."

Q: Where did the term Abominable Snowman come from?

A: One of the many names for the Yeti in popular culture is the Abominable Snowman. This originated from a 1921 expedition funded by the Royal Geographical Society and the Alpine Club called the Mount Everest Reconnaissance Expedition. Their aim was to find a good route for a Mount Everest climb. Some tracks found in the snow, likely from wolves, prompted some of the local Sherpas to talk about the hairy wild men. Henry Newman, a journalist who interviewed the group in Darjeeling, India, latched onto talk of the wild men, and a Tibetan member of the group called them the Metoh Kangmi, which the journalist mistranslated as "Abominable Snowmen." The term has been used interchangeably with the word "Yeti" in English-speaking countries ever since.

Q: What ethnic group is often conflated with a profession?

A: "Sherpa" is often referred to by Westerners as the name of a profession of guiding people up the Himalayan mountains in Tibet. Although there are indeed many Sherpas who make their living as mountain guides (since many people want the adventure of climbing the highest peaks in the world), Sherpa is actually an ethnic group and the language of that group. There are around 150,000 Sherpas in the world (mostly in Tibet), and only a small percentage of them take people on mountain tours for a living.

Q: What reputable organization posted pictures of supposed fresh Yeti footprints to Twitter in 2019?

A: The official Twitter account of the Indian Army has a handle of @adgpi and a bio that reads "Additional Directorate

General of Public Information, IHQ of MoD (Army)." On April 9, 2019, this account posted a picture of the Indian Army Mountaineering Expedition Team along with pictures of what they say are thirty-two-inch by fifteen-inch footprints found close to their Makalu Base Camp, which the post indicates is outside of the normal Yeti sighting area of Makalu Barun National Park. The footprints were spotted when the group was out on a routine expedition to reach the peak of Mount Makalu.

Q: What is the oldest documented hairy hominid cryptid?

A: Like most regions, China has its own hairy ape-man cryptid: the Yeren, meaning "wild man." It is mentioned in documents as early as 500 BCE, making it the earliest documented type of Yeti or Bigfoot creature on Earth. The Yeren is said to inhabit the Hubei province in northwestern China, whose Shennongjia forest is the largest forest in China, with a climate that ranges from warm temperate to subtropical, and home to a vast array of rare flora and fauna, including the giant salamander and the golden snub-nosed monkey. People who have reported sightings describe the Yeren as a tall, bipedal cryptid with reddish-brown hair and large feet. Although early accounts painted it as an aggressive creature, recent accounts usually describe a more docile demeanor.

Q: What hairy hominid is said to reside in northern Queensland in Australia?

A: The Yowie is a hair-covered bipedal cryptid with long arms and an apelike face, said to stand anywhere from five to ten feet tall and described variously as having reddish-brown, black, or white hair. Modern sightings have been reported from 1790 to present, but tales of the Yowie originate with the aboriginal Kuku Yalanji tribe, which is said to have coexisted with the Yowie for centuries. Cave art in the area even depicts what look like tall, hairy hominids along with humans.

Q: What hairy bipedal cryptid has reportedly been sighted in Northeast India?

A: There have been several reported sightings of a Yeti or Sasquatch type of creature in the Garo Hills in the state of Meghalaya. The cryptid is referred to as Mande Barung, meaning "mane of the jungle," and it is said to be half-man, half-ape, with red hair, and to stand as high as ten feet tall.

Q: What hairy mythological creature is said to roam the Pyrenees forests?

A: The Basque are a people who mostly inhabit an area in the western Pyrenees mountains and along the Bay of Biscay, a region that is partially in France and partially in Spain. Although some Basque people no longer speak their original language, many still speak the non-Indo-European Basque language and retain mythology from the earlier animist Basque religion, before they converted to Christianity in the tenth century. And one creature that survives in Basque folklore is the Basajaun, a shaggy cave-dwelling hominid said to roam the forests around the Pyrenees mountains. Its name means "lord of the forest," and it is said that the creature helps shepherds by protecting sheep from predators and by warning them of oncoming storms. The Basajaun was also said to have taught men how to make and use tools for farming and milling. See Chapter Seven for one intriguing theory on who the Basajaun might really have been.

Q: What hairy hominid is said to reside in the Altai, Caucasus, and Pamir mountains in Central Asia?

A: The Almas (or plural Almasty) is a cryptid said to inhabit the Altai, Caucasus, and Pamir mountain areas of Mongolia. Almasty are described as a humanlike bipedal creatures with red or brown hair all over except on their faces and hands. Almasty are sometimes said to resemble Neanderthal man, a humanlike species that shared a close common ancestor with Homo sapiens (us) and lived in Eurasia until around 40,000 years ago—as far as we know. Some believe that the Almasty are surviving members of this ancient hominid species, which if true would mean they didn't die out when we thought. Sightings of Almasty have been reported for centuries. In fact, there have been reports of strange, hairy, humanlike creatures in the region dating back thousands of years.

Q: What hairy cryptid is said to roam mountains between the territories of the Himalayan Yeti and the Central Asian Almasty?

A: The Barmanu, sometimes spelled Barmanou, is a hairy hominid cryptid said to live in the Hindu Kush and Karakoram mountain range in northern Pakistan. Long a creature of the area's folklore, this ape-man has reportedly been spotted by shepherds and others in the Chitral District and was described by some to be wearing animal skins. The Barmanu and Almas are thought to be local names for the same type of creature.

Q: What cryptid did a North Vietnamese general have an area surveyed for during the Vietnam War?

A: The Nguoi Rung ("forest people" in Vietnamese) is a cryptid that is said to inhabit areas at the borders of Vietnam,

Laos, and Cambodia. The creature is reported to be bipedal and covered in hair (with hair color reported as brown, black, or gray) and to possess the ability to climb trees effortlessly. There have been numerous sightings, including during the Vietnam War, which prompted North Vietnamese general Hoàng Minh Thảo to order a scientific expedition into the area north of Kontum in 1974 while the war was still raging. The party didn't find the Nguoi Rung but did return with two elephants. In 1982, Professor Tran Hong Viet made a cast of a footprint in the area that was wider than a typical human foot and had longer toes, but like all cryptids to date, no specimens have been captured, alive or dead.

Q: **What cryptid prompted the creation of a special government post in a Japanese town?**

A: On July 20, 1970, a man reported seeing a hairy creature that walked upright while he was driving a pickup in the mountains of Saijo, Japan, in the Hiroshima Prefecture (which is now the Saijocho district in the city of Shobara). Others came forward with similar stories of a creature who stood a little over five feet tall, covered in reddish hair, with a face shaped somewhat like an upside-down triangle. The creature was dubbed Hibagon (named for Mount Hiba). The media attention was so intense that the town created a government position for one person to investigate Hibagon sightings and handle media inquiries. Some believed Hibagon to be an escaped gorilla from a zoo in Hiroshima and others a Hiba mountain spirit sent to haunt them because of local construction defacing the area. The sightings stopped by 1975, and the mystery was never solved.

Q: What hairy cryptid is said to inhabit the rainforest in Sumatra?

A: Sumatra, an island in western Indonesia, has its own hairy man-ape: a four-foot-tall bipedal creature covered in dark hair (except for perhaps the face) and dubbed Orang Pendek (meaning "short person"). Orang Pendek is said to inhabit the Kerinci Seblat National Park, which is a rainforest in western Sumatra, and to sometimes wander into the more developed areas nearby in search of food (which they are said to steal from local crops).

Q: What mysterious humanlike beings are said to inhabit an Indonesian island?

A: Orang Pendek is not the only unproven inhabitant of the islands of Indonesia. Local folklore has it that a three-and-a-half-foot-tall race of people called the Ebu Gogo inhabits the island of Flores, where incidentally just such a skeleton was found in 2003 and dubbed *Homo floresiensis*. This smaller human relative is thought to have existed in the area until about 50,000 years ago. A similar race of three-foot-tall hominids called Orang Kardil (or "tiny men") is said to inhabit the jungles of Sumatra, the stomping grounds of the Orang Pendek.

Q: What governmental entity created a commission to study "Snowmen"?

A: In 1958, the Academy of Sciences of the Soviet Union created a commission to look into the Almas (a Yeti-type creature of the area) and even funded a "Snowman" expedition that same year into the Pamir Mountains, where there had been lots of reported sightings of the creatures. Soviet scientist Dr. Boris F. Porshnev hypothesized that these hairy snowmen might be surviving Neanderthal men. See Chapter Nine to learn more about one of the explorers of the expedition who had a long and fruitful life.

Q: What humanlike cryptid is said to roam the wilderness of Canada's Northwest Territories?

A: The Nuk-luk is a cryptid that is said to inhabit the area surrounding Nahanni Butte in the Northwest Territories region of Canada. The Nuk-luk is a hominid like Sasquatch, but unlike Sasquatch, people who claimed to have seen the creature described it as more humanlike, similar to a Neanderthal man, around five feet tall, and sporting a long beard. The first sighting was reported in April 1964 by John Baptist, an aboriginal man from the Fort Liard area, along with a group of trappers, who all happened upon a naked manlike creature with a long beard who growled at them and ran off. A second sighting occurred in June of that year, when a fourteen-year-old boy named Jerry and his dad (name unknown) went outside at night to see why their dog was barking. They reportedly found a five-foot-tall bipedal hominid mostly covered in dark hair, with a long beard and a tan face. They claimed that unlike its naked counterpart, it carried a stone club and wore a moose-skin loincloth and boots!

Q: What cryptid reportedly attacked two people in the Philippines in 2008?

A: The Amomongo is a white, hairy, apelike creature around five and a half feet tall with long, sharp nails or claws, reputed to live in the Philippines. In June 2008 in the barangay of Sag-ang, La Castellana, in the province of Negros Occidental, two men and a few animals were reportedly attacked by a creature fitting this description. Some believe the Amomongo to be an albino gorilla or other ape, but there are no known apes native to the Philippines. The area is near the cave-filled Mount Kanlaon, where the creature is thought to dwell.

Q: What creature supposedly attacked a number of people in Delhi in May 2001?

A: For around two weeks in May 2001 in Delhi, the capital of India, around twenty people were reportedly pounced on, bitten, and scratched by a creature described as anywhere from three to six feet tall with a face like a monkey's. Some described it as having dark fur, and others a leather jacket, motorcycle helmet, and sunglasses. Some said it had iron claws and teeth, and in some accounts it had glowing red eyes. At least one mentioned roller skates. All the attacks occurred in the middle of the night in poor areas of the city, which at the time was going through a heat wave and having rolling blackouts, causing many people to sleep outside. The panic caused by the reported attacks led to armed mobs patrolling the streets, at least one man being beaten by a mob after accusations that he was the Monkey Man, and at least two deaths: one man who fell off a roof after someone yelled that the creature was nearby, and a pregnant woman who panicked and fell down the stairs. A reward was offered for tips on the attacker, leading to even more sightings and hoax reports. This creature was dubbed the Monkey Man. See Chapter Seven for what might account for this spate of attacks.

Q: What cryptid is associated with a specific mountainous area in Scotland?

A: The Scottish cryptid Am Fear Liath Mor, also referred to as Ferlas Mor, or the Big Gray Man, seems to be akin to the ubiquitous hairy hominids like the Yeti reported all over the world, but with some notable differences. The Big Gray Man is described as a bipedal creature covered in hair (in this case, short gray hair) who stands anywhere from ten to twenty feet high, with an oversized head and neck, pointy ears, long legs, and long talon-tipped toes. The creature is usually said to be shrouded in mist and to induce panic in anyone who encounters it. There have been several reports from mountaineers over the years climbing the Scottish mountain Ben Macdui (the second highest mountain in Scotland), and one climbing nearby Braeriach (the third highest), of hearing footsteps behind them that seem to be of a much longer stride than the climbers and being overtaken by a great panic. Some have also heard music, and some have even seen what looked like the tall figure of Am Fear Liath Mor in the mist behind them. In all cases, when the climbers descended the mountain, the figure appeared to be gone. See Chapter Seven for phenomena that could explain the Big Gray Man and other tall, spectral mountain creatures.

Q: What shaggy cryptid is said to make appearances in eastern Tennessee?

A: The Tennessee Wildman is a shaggy ape-man with light-brown or light-red hair that has been reported in eastern Tennessee since the 1970s. Most sightings occurred in the woods or by homeowners with houses bordering the woods. One eyewitness reported a powerful rotten smell, another a nine-foot-tall hominid in a tree, and another reported not seeing anything, but hearing a caveman-like grunting noise followed by bipedal footsteps.

Q: What is the hairy ape-man of Tajikistan?

A: The Golub-Yavan is an ape-man reported in eastern Tajikistan, with dark or reddish-gray hair over most of its body. It may be the local equivalent to the Almas of Central Asia. It is often described as more of a hairy Neanderthal type than a Bigfoot-type cryptid, standing five to six and a half feet tall, with hair over much of its body, but not on its face, buttocks, palms, or feet.

Q: What hairy hominid is reported in Kazakhstan?

A: The Ksy-Gyik is a hairy, bipedal Neanderthal-like creature reported in the mountainous areas of Kazakhstan and Kyrgyzstan. It is said to stand around five feet tall and to have blondish to dark-brown hair with a large jaw and a hump at the back of its neck. It is possibly a local variation of the Almas.

Q: What group of small, hairy hominids were reportedly wiped out in Sri Lanka in the late 1700s?

A: In Sri Lanka there are tales of a now extinct group of small, three-foot-tall or so, hairy ape-men called the Nittaewo, who walked upright, were either fully covered or partially covered in reddish hair, and had claws on their feet. The Nittaewo apparently vexed the Vedda people of the area so much that they eradicated the small ape-men. Early twentieth-century Western explorers were told by locals that in 1775 the Vedda drove the last remaining Nittaewo into a cave and burned a fire at the entrance for three days until they all suffocated and died.

Q: What hairy creature with a cute name was first sighted in the early 1970s in the town of Louisiana, Missouri?

A: In 1972, when playing outside, the children of the Harrison family of Louisiana, Missouri, reportedly saw a tall, hairy hominid come out of the woods holding either an infant creature or a dead animal. Reports of these and other sightings were carried by the local papers and TV networks, which dubbed the creature Momo (a shortened form of Missouri Monster). People who claimed to have seen Momo described it as a six- to seven-foot-tall bipedal creature covered in hair, and some said it had glowing red eyes. Momo footprints were reported to show only three toes rather than the usual four of the typically reported Bigfoot print.

Q: What hairy hominid reportedly stalks the southwestern slope of the Colorado Plateau in Arizona?

A: The Mogollon (pronounced mo-gee-on) Rim in Arizona covers an approximately two-hundred-mile area on the southwestern slope of the Colorado Plateau, near the famous Grand Canyon. The Mogollon Rim is reportedly home to its own Bigfoot-like creature. The first sighting was in 1903, when I. W. Stevens was on vacation in the area and reported that he happened upon large footprints, and then saw a wild man with green eyes, two-inch claws on its fingers, white hair covering his body, and a pungent odor. The creature was dubbed the Mogollon Monster, and a number of sightings have been reported since then, including one by a future cryptozoologist (see Chapter Nine).

Q: What hairy hominid is said to roam near Fouke, Arkansas?

A: The state of Arkansas has its own famous Sasquatch-like hairy hominid: the Fouke Monster, also known as the Boggy Creek Monster. It is said to be a bipedal creature standing anywhere from seven to ten feet tall, with red eyes and long, dark hair, that roams the creeks from the area of the Sulphur River Bottoms to Fouke, Arkansas. It is also noted for its pungent odor. Sightings of the creature have been reported in the area from 1908 to recently, with the creature getting a good bit of news media attention in the early 1970s, when it also got its own movie. See Chapter Ten for more.

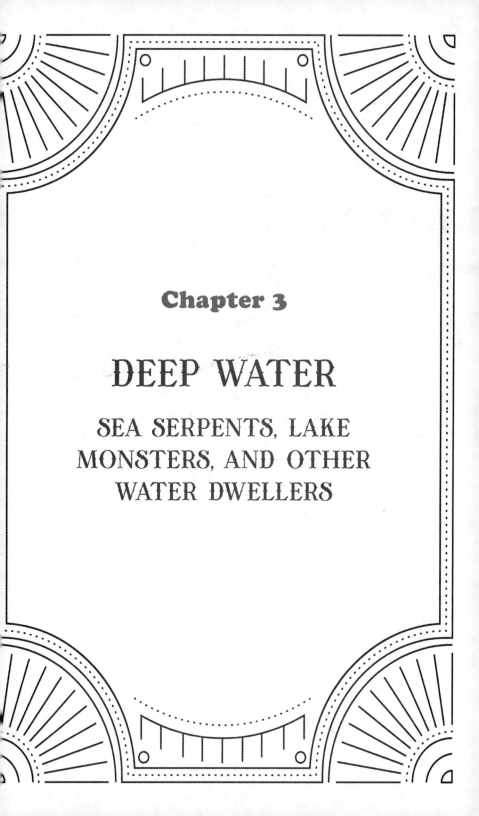

Chapter 3

DEEP WATER

SEA SERPENTS, LAKE MONSTERS, AND OTHER WATER DWELLERS

Q: What creature of Mexican mythology was the mascot of a king?

A: The Ahuizotl is a mythical creature that is said to inhabit the waterways of Mexico. The beast is described as a black-fur-covered aquatic animal somewhat like a dog, with pointed ears, four legs with clawed feet, and (unlike a dog) a long tail with a hand at the end. It is said to use this tail-hand to grab people who get close to the water and drag them under to drown. In some tellings, it can mimic the cry of a child to lure people toward the water. It also apparently likes to feast on people's eyes, nails, and teeth. The Ahuizotl is said to be a protector of the waterways and the fish within them, and thus is known for attacking fishermen.

Ahuizotl was also the mascot of the human Aztec ruler Ahuitzotl, eighth king of Tenochtitlan (now in modern-day Mexico), who ruled from 1486 to 1502 (CE), expanded the Aztec empire, and is said to have sacrificed as many as 20,000 prisoners of war during a four-day ritual to dedicate his new temple.

Q: What ancient cave painting makes some believe there may have been walruses in Africa?

A: In a cave in Brakfontein in South Africa, there are ancient cave paintings of animals. One of these animals is brown and black with some red spots, four limbs (possibly flippers), a long tail that flattens and widens at the end, and two tusks. To some, it resembles a walrus. Add to that the mystery tusk bought in a market in Addis Ababa in 1904 by French zoologist Henri Neuville and Baron Maurice de Rothschild, and one has the makings of a cryptozoological hypothesis. Neuville was apparently told by multiple Somalians that similar tusks came from a large aquatic animal of some East African lakes whose tusks curved downward. Bernard Heuvelmans suggested it could be from an unknown amphibious elephant. In the early 1900s, some European explorers gathered stories of a two-tusked water creature somewhat like a walrus called a dingonek (or sometimes water lion), and in 1907, one of the explorers even claimed to have seen one and attempted to shoot it.

Q: What Norwegian creature of mythology was first described by a king?

A: The fearsome sea monster the Kraken, said to bring down entire ships, made its first appearance in Norwegian lore in a manuscript written in 1180 by none other than King Sverre of Norway.

Q: What was the earliest recorded sea serpent sighting in North America?

A: In 1639, a large sea serpent, coiled on a rock at Cape Ann off the coast of Massachusetts, was reportedly spotted by two Englishmen and two First Nations people who drifted by it in a boat. The area, near Gloucester, Massachusetts, later became well known for multiple sea serpent sightings. Read on to find out about these encounters!

Q: What sea serpent has been reported off the coast of Maine since the 1700s?

A: Maine has had a number of sea-serpent sightings in its coastal bays since at least 1751. The state's Casco Bay Serpent was nicknamed "Cassie" by Loren Coleman in an article in the

May 1986 edition of *Portland Monthly* that detailed sightings from 1779 to present.

Q: **What sea serpent amazed onlookers off the coast of Massachusetts in the 1800s?**

A: In 1817, 1819, 1833, and 1877, there were numerous sightings of a huge sea creature off the coast of Massachusetts in the Gloucester Harbor and Nahant Bay areas. The behemoth was reported as measuring anywhere from forty-five to one hundred feet long and having many humps and a head the size of a horse's, with a spear-like horn protruding from it. The creature seemed to move up and down in an undulating motion rather than side to side like a serpent, swam very fast, could dive suddenly under the water without turning its body, and would sometimes float stationary for hours. Hundreds of eyewitnesses saw the creature. It drew the attention of journalists and scientists, and the Linnaean Society of New England dubbed it *Scoliophis Atlanticus*, although the creature was more popularly known as the Gloucester Sea Serpent. See Chapter Seven to find out a more likely culprit for the sightings.

Q: **What creature of lore was said to disguise itself as an island to lure unsuspecting sailors?**

A: The aspidochelone is a creature found in Greek mythology and medieval bestiaries, sometimes described as a huge fish or whale or crocodile-like monster, and sometimes as a large sea turtle. The aspidochelone was said to rest with its back sticking out of the water, making unsuspecting sailors think it was a small island or rock. They would lay anchor, disembark, and set up a campfire to cook. The creature, feeling the heat of the flames, would dive, knocking the sailors off its back and dragging their ship into the sea. An Old English poem calls the creature Fastitocalon (check out Chapter Ten to find out more about this ancient work).

Q: What aquatic cryptid drew the attention of at least one prominent religious leader?

A: In 1868, the *Deseret News* printed accounts of recent sightings of an aquatic creature, or sometimes multiple aquatic creatures, in Bear Lake at the border of Utah and Idaho in what is now Rich County, Utah (at the time Utah was still a territory rather than an official state). Described by some as similar to a crocodile and by others like a dinosaur, the creature was dubbed the Bear Lake Monster (or monsters, as the case may be). And the story drew the attention of none other than Brigham Young, second head of the then nascent Church of Jesus Christ of Latter-day Saints (the Mormon church), the founder of Salt Lake City, and the first governor of the Utah Territory. Young traveled to the area to talk to locals, and later suggested providing them with a rope to catch whatever they were seeing in the lake, although nothing came of it. There have been additional sightings as recently as 2002. Although still usually referred to as the Bear Lake Monster, a contest was held among schoolchildren during the 1996 Raspberry Days festival, and the name Isabella (chosen by eight-year-old Amanda Price) won.

Q: What other cryptid do some believe is connected to Utah's Bear Lake Monster?

A: The Bear Lake Monster (aka Isabella) is a cryptid in Utah described by some as looking like the Loch Ness Monster. But some take the idea that they are similar even further and believe that they are, indeed, the same creature. Their hypothesis is that Nessie travels back and forth between Loch Ness in Scotland and Bear Lake in Utah via a subterranean channel. That's quite a trip!

Q: What sea monster can reportedly be attracted by tapping on the inside of a boat?

A: The Tizheruk (also called the Palraiyuk) is a beast of Inuit mythology reported to live off the coasts of King Island and the island of Nunivak in Alaska. It is described as a fifteen-or-so-foot-long carnivorous sea creature with a horned wolflike head, a long neck, and a tail that ends in a flipper. It is said to occasionally kill people by flipping boats or snatching them off piers. In 2009, footage purported to be of the creature was taken by a fisherman, although it was filmed in the rain and is quite grainy. In Inuit lore, the Tizheruk can be attracted by tapping on the inside hull of a boat. This has led some cryptozoologists to speculate that it might be some unknown Arctic counterpart to the Antarctic leopard seal *Hydrurga leptonyx*, which can be attracted by tapping on the hull of a boat.

Q: What infrastructure project led to a series of water monster sightings?

A: Loch Ness is the largest of a series of lakes that run through the Great Glen in Scotland. At over twenty miles long, around a mile wide, and over seven hundred feet deep, it is the largest body of freshwater in not only Scotland, but in Great Britain. In the early 1930s, a road running alongside Loch Ness was expanded. As a result, the surrounding area was cleared, and the view of the lake from the road was improved. In April 1933, a couple reported seeing a large animal in the lake that some described as a monster, and a number of other sightings followed. Commonly known as Nessie, the creature is usually described as looking like an aquatic dinosaur and is said to be capable of causing large waves and whirlpools in the water. Nessie is one of the most well-known cryptids the world over.

Q: What famous photographs made people believers in Nessie?

A: The first famous photograph of what is purported to be the Loch Ness Monster (aka Nessie) was taken in November 1933 by Hugh Gray, an employee of British Aluminum Company. He said he was walking home from church along the lake when he spotted Nessie and stopped to take several photos. Only one showed anything. It is a blurry, indistinct photograph of something on the lake's surface.

Another famous photograph was published by the *Daily Mail* in April 1934, purportedly taken by Lieutenant Colonel Robert Kenneth Wilson, who was a surgeon and gynecologist, which led to the photo often being referred to as the "surgeon's photograph." It showed a dark creature on the surface of the lake with a long, curved neck and dinosaur-like head sticking out of the water, and many took this to be definitive proof of the existence of Nessie. But there was more to the story. See Chapter Eight to find out what the picture *really* showed.

Q: What large cryptid is said to inhabit lakes in the Congo Basin?

A: In 1913, German American cryptozoologist Willy Otto Oskar Ley wrote of a report from German officer Ludwig Freiherr von Stein zu Lausnitz recounting tales from locals of (at the time) the German colony of Kamerun (now the country of Cameroon). Mokele-Mbembe was described as a large reptilian creature with a long, flexible neck and long tail that inhabited the region's swampy lakes. Despite being an herbivore, the cryptid reportedly killed anyone who got too close. The descriptions were taken to resemble a bronto-saurus (now called "apatosaurus"), and despite a lack of any physical evidence, some people still believe and search for Mokele-Mbembe to this day.

Q: What Idaho lake cryptid got a name change in the 1950s?

A: The Indigenous people of what is now Valley County, Idaho, have stories of an evil spirit living in Big Payette Lake, a five-thousand-acre lake in McCall, Idaho. Sightings of a lake creature began with loggers in 1920, who saw what they thought was a huge log floating in the water. When the "log" started to undulate, they fled the area. In subsequent sightings in 1944 and 1946, eyewitnesses described a thirty-five-foot-long dinosaur-like creature with a periscope-shaped head, protruding jaw, camel-like humps, and shell-like skin, which left a wake like a boat and disappeared by diving underwa-ter. Starting with these reports, the media called the creature Slimy Slim. Sightings continued, and in 1954, the *Star-News* held a contest to pick a better name for the beast. A contes-tant from Virginia suggested Sharlie, based on a catchphrase from *The Jack Pearl Show*, a radio show that started in 1933, and in which Jack Pearl played Baron von Munchausen and often said "Vas you der, Sharlie?" ("Were you there, Sharlie?") when his sidekick Sharlie doubted one of his stories. And the name Sharlie was the winner, and Slimy Slim was no more!

Q: What water creature is said to swim in the lake of a town in Sweden?

A: In the province of Jämtland in Sweden, there have been hundreds of sightings of the Storsjöodjuret ("the Great Lake Monster") swimming in Storsjön ("the Great Lake"), the fifth largest lake in Sweden, dating all the way back to 1635. The creature is described as looking like an overturned boat or a log with humps, its color ranging from yellow to black, with a horselike head, a long neck, big eyes, a big mouth, sometimes with feet, and measuring anywhere from nine to thirty-nine feet long. Danish zoologist and cryptozoologist Lars Thomas believes that most of the lake monster sightings in Storsjön are actually of swimming moose, although some still believe otherwise.

Q: What monster is reputed to live in Okanagan Lake in British Columbia?

A: Ogopogo is a lake monster said to dwell in eighty-four-mile-long Okanagan Lake in the British Columbia, Canada. It is most often described as a sea serpent–like creature with multiple humps, a head like a horse or snake, and green or black skin, although some say it can change color. Sixteen percent of British Columbians reportedly believe Ogopogo to be real. A statue of the cryptid greets visitors along the Waterfront Boardwalk in the lakeside town of Kelowna.

Q: From what Indigenous spirit was Ogopogo appropriated?

A: In Syilx (or Okanagan) and Secwépemc tales, N'ha-a-itk (pronounced "n-ha-ha-it-koo") is a sacred spirit of the lake that protects the Okanagan Valley. The spirit is said to live on Rattlesnake Island. The Syilx people, who have inhabited the area for 12,000 years or more, make offerings of sage, tobacco, and salmon to the spirit.

Q: **What potential cousin of Ogopogo has been sighted off the coast of the Pacific Northwest in North America?**

A: Ogopogo (said to inhabit Okanagan Lake) isn't the only sea monster to have been sighted in the British Columbia area. A creature fitting a similar description has been spotted all over the Pacific Northwest coast, from Alaska to California. In the 1930s, a Victoria, British Columbia, newspaper gave the creature the name Cadborosaurus for the area in which it has been most frequently sighted: Cadboro Bay near Victoria. The beast, which, like Ogopogo, is said to have a long serpentine body with humps sticking out of the water and a head like a horse, is more affectionately referred to as Caddy.

Q: **What cryptid did Greenpeace declare an endangered species in the 1980s?**

A: In the 1980s, a tourism group offered $1 million to anyone who could provide proof of the existence of Ogopogo in Okanagan Lake. Greenpeace, being in the business of protecting sea life, declared Ogopogo an endangered species and asked that people photograph (rather than capture or kill) the creature.

Q: **What cryptid may have been named in part for a Walt Kelly cartoon?**

A: *Pogo* was a comic strip by cartoonist Walt Kelly that ran from 1948 to 1975. In 1952, Kelly released a book called *I Go Pogo*, in which the title character, Pogo, an opossum, runs for president of the United States using the slogan "I

Go Pogo." That, in combination with the reputed Ogopogo aquatic cryptid of Okanagan Lake in British Columbia, may have served as inspiration for another lake monster: Igopogo of Lake Simcoe, Ontario. Igopogo is said to be a large seal-like aquatic creature with a strange-looking doglike head.

Q: What cryptid reportedly calls Lake Champlain home?

A: Lake Champlain is the largest lake in the Adirondack Mountain area in Upstate New York. And like many large lakes, there have been reports of a lake monster, this one dubbed Champ. The Abenaki and Iroquois people of the area have legends of a serpentine creature in the lake, which they call Gitaskog or Tatoskok. Once European explorers showed up and were warned of the creature, regular sightings began to be reported and continue to this day. In 1819, a Captain Crum claimed to have seen a 187-foot-long black monster with a white star on its sea-horse-like head in the lake. There have been resolutions passed in three places to protect the creature, whether it exists or not: the city of Port Henry, New York; the House of the state of Vermont, and the New York State Assembly and Senate.

Q: What creature is said to inhabit Lake Tahoe?

A: Lake Tahoe is a freshwater lake at the border of Nevada and California, and, at 1,645 feet deep, is the second deepest lake in the United States. But that's not Lake Tahoe's only claim to fame. Like many deep lakes, Lake Tahoe has its own famous aquatic monster. While Loch Ness has Nessie, Lake Tahoe has Tessie. There is no clear description of Tahoe Tessie, but there have been numerous sightings of either something unseen creating a wake on the surface of the water or a large creature at least ten feet long beneath the surface. An especially high number of sightings were reported in the 1980s.

Q: What large cryptid is said to call Lake Erie home?

A: Lake Erie has its own cryptid, whose first known sighting was reported in 1793 by the captain of sailboat *Felicity* near the Lake Erie islands of the South Bay. And in the grand tradition of dinosaur-like lake monsters in English-speaking areas, its name rhymes with the nicknames of its Loch Ness and Lake Tahoe counterparts: Nessie and Tessie. Dubbed South Bay Bessie (aka the Lake Erie Monster, or the Great Serpent of Lake Erie), the monster is described as a serpentine and reptilian creature (although sometimes with a doglike head) measuring over five meters (sixteen feet) long, with silver or copper skin and fins or flippers.

Q: What Indigenous water spirit is Lake Erie's Bessie likely based on?

A: Like many cryptids, South Bay Bessie can trace its origins to First Nations folklore. The Iroquois and other local tribes have tales of a fire-and-poison-breathing serpentine water spirit of Lake Erie known as Oniare (pronounced "own-year-eh"), which means "snake" in the Mohawk language.

Q: What cryptid left bite marks on swimmers at Lake Erie?

A: South Bay Bessie isn't the only mysterious creature in Lake Erie. In 2001, three swimmers over two days (one of them a child) entered the waters at the pump house beach area near Port Dover on Lake Erie in Canada only to be driven out by painful attacks. The wounds consisted of small punctures situated in the shape of an open jaw—bite marks!

Some believed the attacks were released piranha, or even baby Bessies! The biting creature was dubbed the Lake Erie Chomper. See Chapter Seven to find out the likely culprit.

Q: **What two lake monsters are said to reside in Japan?**

A: Scotland has Nessie, the US has Bessie and Tessie, and Japan has Issie-kun and Kusshi (or Kussie)! Issie, also called Isshi, was spotted in 1978 by around twenty people who said they saw a black two-humped creature a few meters in length in Lake Ikeda, which is on Kyushu Island in Kagoshima Prefecture, Japan. Toshiaki Matsuhara took a photo of something in the lake later that year, but in the grand tradition of cryptid photos, it's hard to make out exactly what it is. Kusshi was also spotted in the 1970s by over two dozen people in Lake Kussharo in Hokkaido in northern Japan. Both creatures have become mascots for their respective areas. Kyushu Island has several cartoonish statues of Issie along its shore.

Q: **What sea creature is called "the Friendly Monster" by locals?**

A: Cape Greco off the coast of the resort town of Ayia Napa, which is on the southeastern shores of the island nation of Cypress, is reportedly home to a sea monster that is alternately described to be like a serpent or a crocodile. There have been reported sightings, but as with many cryptids, no photographic or scientific evidence exists. The creature is a tourism draw, however. And it isn't described as in any way dangerous, except sometimes to fishermen's nets. In fact, local residents refer to the creature as O Filikos Teras, which means "the Friendly Monster."

Q: What plank-spined water creature was said to possibly inhabit the waters of the Congo?

A: Mbielu-Mbielu-Mbielu was reportedly described by a local to cryptozoologist Roy Mackal as a creature who was only seen with its back sticking out of the water, but its back included protruding planks and was also often covered with algae. The person described it after seeing a stegosaurus in a book of Mackal's and said it looked similar. This is apparently the only known account of the creature, however.

Q: What sea creature reportedly haunts the waters around Fort King George in the US state of Georgia?

A: The Altamaha-ha (also called Altie for short) is a sea monster said to live in the waters at the mouth of the Altamaha River near Fort King George near Darien, Georgia. The Altamaha-ha is often described as a thirty-foot-long green serpentine creature with a horselike head, sometimes with a crocodile-like snout, bulging eyes, sharp teeth, a body somewhat like a sturgeon, two flippers, a bony ridge down its back, and a long tail ending in a flipper. The creature is also said to make a hissing noise.

The first reported sighting was in an account in a Darien newspaper in the 1820s, in which a sea captain described a creature that attacked his ship.

But the legend of the Altamaha-ha reportedly began much earlier with the Lower Muscogee (also known as Creek) First Nations tribe that used to have a large population in the area until their forced removal and relocation (of those who didn't die along the way) to Oklahoma in the 1830s as part of a shameful two-decades-long government operation now known as the Trail of Tears.

The Darien, Georgia, Welcome Center displays a statue of the creature, which was sculpted by artist Rick Spears in 2009.

Q: What monster is said to have taken up residence in an artificial lake in North Carolina?

A: Lake Norman has only existed since the construction of the Cowans Ford Dam, which took place from 1959 to 1964. And since then, there have been dozens of monster sightings, during which people reported seeing anything from a long, dark shape under the surface to a crocodile-like creature to a Loch Ness–style dinosaur. The creature, whatever its form, has been dubbed the Lake Norman Monster (or Normie for short).

Q: What type of creature is said to drown people in three lakes in Oklahoma?

A: Lake Oolagah, Lake Tenkiller, and Lake Thunderbird (the latter itself bearing the name of another cryptid) are said to be home to a creature called the Oklahoma Octopus. Unlike the typical octopus (which dwells in saltwater), this freshwater creature is described as horse-sized, with reddish-brown skin and long tentacles. All three of the lakes the Oklahoma Octopus is said to call home were made in the middle of the twentieth century by damming up rivers, and their waters are typically calm. But an uptick of drownings in the twenty-first century have been blamed by some on the tentacled cryptid.

Q: What aquatic creature reportedly haunted the waters at the mouth of Oregon's Columbia River in the 1930s?

A: The Columbia Bar Sea Serpent (aka Colossal Claude) is a cryptid that was spotted off the coast of Oregon at the mouth of the Columbia River several times in the 1930s. The first reported sighting occurred in March 1934, when the crews of two lightships (the *Columbia River* and the *Rose*) reported seeing a forty-foot sea serpent with a long neck, a round body, a tail, and a head either like that of a camel or of a snake, depending on which crew member you asked. Claude appeared again in 1937, when the captain of the fishing trawler *Viv* described seeing a forty-foot-long creature with a body four feet in diameter and the head of an oversized horse, and the added detail that the creature was covered in tan hair. Not long after, a couple on a beach spotted what they said looked like a giraffe neck and head sticking fifteen feet out of the water attached to what they thought was a fifty-five-foot-long creature. In 1939, the creature was spotted by the crew of the fishing boat *Argo*, whose captain described it as having a neck that stuck ten feet out of the water with a camel-like head and gray fur all over. He said the beast ate a twenty-pound halibut off their fishing lines. Most of the sightings took place during the Chinook salmon season in the spring and ended entirely within a few years of the *Argo* sighting, perhaps because construction of a dam depleted the salmon population in the area.

Q: **What horned creatures are said to inhabit the waters of North America?**

A: There are a number of horned serpent creatures described in the legends of Indigenous peoples of North America, including a water monster said by the Oneida tribe to have slain people on Onondaga Lake near present-day Syracuse, a horned snake said by the Creek people to have inhabited watering holes in Tennessee, another ancient horned serpent said to have killed people on Lake Ontario around the year 700 BCE, and the Alkali Lake Monster of Nebraska (see Chapter

Five, "A Bit of Americana: Regional Cryptids of the US," for more information on the latter). They are all described as huge aquatic snake- or crocodile-like reptiles with horns on their heads. And some made the jump from First Nations legend to sightings, making them cryptids.

Q: **What segmented sea serpent is said to inhabit the tropical waters of Southeast Asia?**

A: Con Rit (Vietnamese for millipede) is a sea serpent reported in the waters of Southeast Asia. It is described as a sixty-foot-long, three-foot-wide sea creature with two-foot-long armored segments that make up the length of its body (thus its comparison to a millipede). It is said to be brown with a yellow underbelly. Cryptozoologist Bernard Heuvelmans gave the Con Rit the scientific name *Cetioscolopendra aeliani*, although to date none have been found or officially classified.

Chapter 4

TAKING FLIGHT

WINGED CREATURES

Q: What North American cryptid is said to have a wingspan of up to seventy feet?

A: The thunderbird is a bird of legend in the mythology of multiple First Nations peoples that was credited with causing thunderstorms. It is usually said that thunderbirds are mostly covered in dark feathers, with a lighter colored head, sometimes white feathers around the neck, and a wingspan up to seventy feet, far greater than that of any bird known to science (the record is the wandering albatross at twelve feet). Thunderbirds are also said to carry off livestock, and the occasional child!

Q: What mysterious winged beast reportedly terrorized a town in Iowa in 1903?

A: Over several days in the fall of 1903 in Van Meter, Iowa, several well-respected men reported seeing a very-fast-flying, odd-smelling, half-man half-beast with bat-like wings, three-toed feet, and a horned head that emitted a beam of light. Several independently attempted to shoot the creature. On the final night, a mob gathered near an old, abandoned coal mine where someone heard the beast. They reportedly found it with a similar but smaller creature (offspring, perhaps?). Both flew away but returned in the morning. The mob opened fire, but gunfire didn't seem to hurt them. The monsters proceeded to climb down the mineshaft, and no one ever saw them again. The creature was dubbed the Van Meter Visitor.

Q: What winged cryptid is named for the sound it makes?

A: In 1925, Dr. Ernest Bartels, the son of a famous ornithologist, was in Java, an island of Indonesia, exploring a waterfall on Mount Salak. According to Bartels, a large bat that he couldn't identify flew over him. He and cryptozoologist Ivan T. Sanderson uncovered sightings of this creature all over western Java. It was described as a gray bat-like creature the size of a one-year-old human child. Some say its head looks more like that of a macaque or other primate. It apparently lives off fish from the rivers. The creature reportedly makes a sound that is something like "Ahooool!" It has thus been dubbed the Ahool.

Q: What flying creature was reportedly sighted by cryptozoologist Ivan T. Sanderson?

A: On a trip through the Assumbo Mountains in Cameroon in 1932, zoologist and early cryptozoologist Ivan T. Sanderson, along with naturalist Gerald Russell, reported being dive-bombed by a black flying creature with sharp teeth around the size of an eagle. People from the area referred to the beast as Olitiau. Sanderson believed it to be a larger than usual hammerhead bat. Read on to find out what other cryptid may or may not be the same creature as Olitiau.

Q: What flying cryptid is alternately described as a huge bat-like creature or an ancient flying reptile?

A: The Kongamato, sometimes called Olitiau or Sasabonsam, is a winged creature said to fly around all over Sub-Saharan Africa. It was described by locals to at least one westerner in the 1920s as a red flying creature with teeth, membranes instead of feathers over its wings, and a wingspan of up to seven feet. More than one western explorer showed local people pictures of pterodactyls and got confirmation that this was the animal. But they apparently didn't show them pictures of bats, which could also fit some of the descriptions. There has been debate between cryptozoologists as to whether the Kongamato is a surviving flying dinosaur or a giant fruit bat. Or whether the Kongamato and Olitiau are two different cryptids.

Q: What winged creature is said to eat small children?

A: The Orang Bati is a cryptid said to inhabit the island of Seram in Indonesia (a member of the Molucca islands). The creature's name apparently means "men with wings" in the Molucca language. Christian missionaries were reportedly told tales of the creature starting in the 1500s. The animal is described as a five-foot, orange, flying, monkey-like creature with bat wings and a long tail. It is said to call a dormant volcano on the island home, where it apparently chows down on the prey it captures—including small children!

Q: What regenerating mythical bird is said to heal wounds with its tears?

A: You may know the phoenix from the Harry Potter book series, in which Professor Dumbledore kept this mythical bird as a pet named Fawkes. The phoenix (from the ancient Greek word *phoinos* meaning "blood red") is a large red bird of ancient mythology that was said to burst into flames at the end of its long life only to be reborn from the ashes. It was also sometimes said to be able to heal people with its tears. Some people believe it exists, or at least once existed, propelling it into the realm of cryptids.

Q: What winged cryptid terrorized teen hunters in Texas in 1981?

A: In 1981, a group of teens drove out of Sundown, Texas, at night in a pickup truck to go rabbit hunting. Sometime after exiting the vehicle to begin the hunt, they saw a large white creature with red eyes and a red chest sitting on a fence. They described it as owl-like but several times larger, with a twelve-foot wingspan, which they noticed when it charged them and chased them back to the truck. The huge bird continued to pursue them all the way into town, scratching at the vehicle and terrifying the three friends who were relegated to riding in the bed of the truck out in the open. One of the victims said that after the encounter, others recounted that they had seen something similar out in the woods.

Q: What NASA location has reportedly been terrorized by a cryptid?

A: According to an account by Desiree Shaw to British crypto-zoologist and ufologist Nicholas Redfern, her father Frank Shaw saw something terrifying at NASA's Johnson Space Center (JSC) in Houston, Texas. According to the story, in 1986 Frank Shaw, an archivist at the facility, was walking to his car one night, looked at one of the large JSC buildings, and saw a dark, winged creature that looked something like a gargoyle perched atop. It spread its wings and flew off as he stared in terror. Shaw told his family, and they all decided not to tell anyone (because who would believe such a thing?). But at some point he confided in his supervisor, who reportedly told him that he wasn't the only one who had seen the terrifying beast. The creature was even a suspect in the deaths of two German shepherds. Shaw's daughter said he was questioned for details and told to tell no one else.

Chapter 5

A BIT OF AMERICANA

REGIONAL CRYPTIDS OF THE US

Q: What Colorado town was reportedly blown up in an effort to destroy a monster?

A: A cryptid called the Slide-Rock Bolter was said to have been sighted in the late 1800s and early 1900s in areas of the Colorado mountains with slopes of more than forty-five degrees. The creature was described as whalelike, with a large head and mouth, small eyes, and a tail with hooks that held it in place up the slope. It would apparently release the hooks and slide down the mountain to devour hapless tourists or animals, and then use the hooks to climb back up the mountain and wait for more prey.

A park ranger reportedly came up with the idea of destroying the monster by setting up a fake decoy tourist full of gunpowder and fulminate caps. The decoy was set up at Lizard Head. The Slide-Rock Bolter came, the dummy exploded, and half the buildings in a mining town called Rico were destroyed by the blast. But on the bright side, the creature hasn't been reported since.

Q: What cryptids are said to be the offspring of escaped mental patients?

A: The woods of Connecticut are reportedly home to creatures referred to as the Melonheads, described as people with bulbous heads, thin limbs, bulging eyes, crooked teeth, and, according to some, a taste for human flesh. Others say, however, they keep to themselves and avoid outsiders (rather than try to eat them), and that they have an enclave on Velvet Street (sometimes called "Dracula Drive") in Trumbull, Connecticut, in Fairfield County. Their appearance is attributed to inbreeding resulting from their isolation from society at large, and there are two prevailing stories about their origins:

one that they descended from a family cast out for accusations of witchcraft, and the other that they descended from the survivors of an asylum that burned down in 1860. There is the distinct possibility that these tales are mean-spirited explanations for people with deformities.

Q: What Connecticut cryptid is it okay to see twice, but the third time's a curse?

A: The Hanging Hills overlooking Meriden, Connecticut, are where the Black Dog reportedly roams. He will apparently follow people and seem like a perfectly normal dog until astonishing the followed person by vanishing. Legend has it that seeing the dog once is fine, as is a second visit, but a third means death. A geologist in the 1890s reported seeing and being followed by the dog. The story goes that he came back a second time and hiked with a friend who had been there and had seen the dog twice before, and on this third visit, the friend fell off a cliff and died. The geologist survived. One can only speculate that he avoided the area henceforth.

Q: What stealthy cryptid could be foiled by drinking alcohol?

A: Logging is a dangerous job, even more so in desolate forests in the 1800s. A legend sprung out of the logging communities of Michigan, Minnesota, and Wisconsin around that time to explain some of the deaths. The Hidebehind was a thin, wraithlike being with a penchant for hiding behind trees and eviscerating unlucky loggers. But it was said to have been repulsed by the smell of alcohol, giving lumberjacks license to imbibe with abandon. (See Chapter Ten for a modern literary incarnation of the Hidebehind.)

Q: For what cryptid was a hunt organized in Glastonbury, Connecticut, in 1939?

A: In January 1939, a hunt was organized to kill the Glawackus (reportedly derived from a combination of the words "Glastonbury" and "wacky") after residents found large feline paw prints, heard terrifying cries, had farm animals or pets attacked, and in some cases saw what looked like either a four-foot-long black cat, dog, or bear roaming the area, sometimes described as having a bushy tail. The hunt was unsuccessful, but a two-mile-long stretch of paw prints was reportedly found east of town the next month. Several subsequent hunts ended with similar results. A new spate of sightings occurred in the 1950s through the late 1960s, including more attacks on farm animals in 1959 in Granby, Connecticut. Sightings continue, although many later accounts have been of orange or yellowish-brown creatures rather than black.

Q: What cryptid is reportedly the cursed child of a New Jersey woman?

A: The Pine Barrens of New Jersey are said to be home of a fearsome cryptid: the Jersey Devil (originally the Leeds Devil). The backstory is that the creature was the thirteenth child born to a Mrs. Leeds in 1735. He came out with some decidedly nonhuman attributes and has since terrorized the area. Descriptions of the beast are all over the place, but it is usually reported as a red monster with horns, wings, and cloven hooves. Sometimes its face is more human, and sometimes more animal-like. The cryptid is often graphically rendered to look like a cartoon illustration of Satan.

Q: What Bigfoot-like cryptid haunts the swamps of Louisiana?

A: The Honey Island Swamp, around the Pearl River in eastern St. Tammany Parish in Louisiana, is a dense and foggy place where, during Prohibition, bootleggers used to hide their goings-on—and possibly the bodies of their rivals! The area is still said to hide another mystery: the Honey Island Swamp Monster. The beast is said to be a seven-foot-tall Bigfoot-like creature covered in gray hair, with the face of a man, large webbed feet, and yellow eyes.

Q: What Louisiana cryptid can be foiled by placing a certain number of items on the windowsill?

A: The rougarou is a Louisiana-based cryptid that originated from medieval French lore. The name is derived partially from the *loup-garou*, the French term for werewolf. The rougarou is described as having the body of a man but the head of a werewolf, and it is said to eat naughty children. Reported ways to become a rougarou are to be subjected to a curse or (as a Catholic) to fail to observe Lent for seven years straight. And the best protection from the beast is apparently math! You are supposed to place thirteen items on your windowsill to keep a rougarou at bay—because the creature can only count to twelve. The rougarou will go away and you'll live to see another day.

Q: What cryptid likely derived from a Pennsylvania Dutch legend?

A: Colonists in Virginia in the 1600s reported seeing a flying creature with a metallic beak and sharp teeth. For hundreds of years it remained unseen, but in 1909, people reported a similar creature with huge wings; a long beak; sharp, hooked talons; and sometimes an eye in the middle of its forehead. This creature was dubbed the Snallygaster. The idea of the Snallygaster likely began as a legend of the German-descended Pennsylvania Dutch (or Pennsylvania Deutsch) people. The name is probably a derivation of *schnelle geist*, meaning "quick spirit," mythological spirits thought to be responsible for minor mischief. But the name Snallygaster became attached to the giant, seemingly deadly bird, whose description varied greatly. Read on to find out why the Snallygaster was resurrected in northern Maryland.

Q: What Appalachian town declared itself a Bigfoot sanctuary in 2014?

A: The Woodbooger is a Bigfoot-like cryptid said to roam the Flag Rock Recreation Area in Norton, Virginia, in the southwestern part of the state, in addition to other nearby areas. After the filming of an episode of *Finding Bigfoot* in and around the city of Norton in 2011, the town erected a statue of the creature and began throwing an annual Woodbooger Festival, which includes a costume contest, a Woodbooger-calling contest, and an organized search for the creature. In October 2014, the City of Norton also declared itself an official Sasquatch, Bigfoot, and Woodbooger sanctuary!

Q: What creature is said to stalk an area in southeast Wisconsin?

A: In 1936, a school night watchman in Jefferson, Wisconsin, saw a six-foot tall, hairy bipedal creature with a head like a wolf's but a body like a man's, digging into an Indigenous burial mound near the school two nights in a row. He said the creature growled at him, then ran off, and that the growl was somewhat beast-like and somewhat humanlike. In the

1980s and 1990s, a spate of sightings occurred about thirty miles away from the original sighting in Elkhorn, Wisconsin, with multiple people reporting a wolflike creature with sharp teeth, pointy ears, and grayish-brown hair, sometimes walking upright and sometimes on all fours. At least one of the apparent werewolf sightings occurred on Bray Road, and the creature was named the Beast of Bray Road.

Q: What cryptid was used by moonshiners to divert prying eyes away from their stills?

A: In the United States, a period of Prohibition on the production and sale of most alcohol was in effect from 1920 to 1933, starting with the passing of the Eighteenth Amendment to the Constitution and ending with the passing of the Twenty-First Amendment, repealing the Eighteenth Amendment. During this time people didn't really stop drinking. The production and sale of alcohol just went underground and fueled the growth of crime organizations, as well as lots of individual still setups where bootleggers made moonshine (a strong, quickly made and un-aged liquor). In Northern Maryland, to keep people, especially law enforcement and federal agents, from investigating the strange screeching and banging noises emanating from stills hidden in the woods and other remote areas, local moonshiners circulated stories that the sounds were caused by the deadly winged Snallygaster! The creature may have been used as an excuse for the odd dead body, as well.

Q: What porcine creature scared teens near a Vermont high school in the 1950s?

A: On Halloween in the village of Northfield, Vermont, in 1951, a teenager named Sam Harris disappeared. Shortly thereafter, other teens reported seeing a white furry creature that walked like a man but had the face of a pig coming out of the brush near the high school, behind which they were hanging out in a sand pit. The kids ran into the school to take shelter from the beast until it was gone. A farmer also reportedly spotted a pig-faced creature rooting around in his trash cans. The creature was dubbed the Northfield Pigman. Legend has it that Harris was either taken by the pigman—or he became the pigman!

Q: What close encounter terrified a family in Kentucky in the 1950s?

A: On August 21, 1955, a family and family friends raced from the family's farmhouse in Kelly, Kentucky, to the Hopkinsville, Kentucky, police station and described a siege on their home by two-and-a-half- to three-and-a-half-foot-tall silver creatures with large heads, large glowing eyes, large floppy ears, arms that almost touched the ground, and fingers with talons, which had apparently appeared after one of the group saw a silver craft land nearby. They fired shots and some of the creatures scurried away, but some remained, at least one at the family matriarch's window. The cryptids were dubbed the Hopkinsville Goblins.

Q: What disaster was reportedly preceded by sightings of a flying creature with red eyes?

A: In 1966 and 1967, sightings of a flying creature that stood the height of a man and had a massive wingspan and glowing red eyes were reported in Point Pleasant, West Virginia. It was said to be capable of flying at high speeds and of causing people to experience feelings of terror. At first it was referred to as a birdman, but the name Mothman later stuck. On December 15, 1967, the Silver Bridge in Point Pleasant collapsed, killing forty-six in the small town of only around three hundred people. Some linked the disaster with the sightings and pointed to the Mothman as a sort of harbinger of doom, an idea possibly encouraged by John Keel's nonfiction book *The Mothman Prophecies*, published in 1975. The story was later made into a fictional movie of the same name starring Richard Gere and Laura Linney, released in 2002.

Q: What supposedly alien cryptid terrified several eyewitnesses in Flatwoods, West Virginia, in the 1950s?

A: On September 12, 1952, in the small town of Flatwoods, West Virginia, in Braxton County, three boys playing in a schoolyard reportedly saw a red light streak across the sky that appeared to land at a farm nearby. They fetched Kathleen May, mother of two of the boys, and went to investigate along with three others, including seventeen-year-old National Guard member Gene Lemon. Lemon reported seeing eyes in a tree, and then a ten-foot-tall monster with a red body, glowing green face, and possibly clawed hands (which were apparently hard to make out due to a surrounding mist). Lemon fell over backward, a dog with the group was said to have run off with his tail between his legs, and one of the kids reportedly wet himself in terror. The creature was dubbed the Flatwoods Monster. A widely circulated artist's rendition of the creature produced just after the original accounts appears partially organic, partially robotic. You can visit the Flatwoods Monster Museum in Sutton, West Virginia.

Q: What governmental entity investigated the Flatwoods Monster?

A: The United States Air Force ran an initiative called Project Blue Book from 1947 to 1969 to investigate unidentified flying objects (UFOs). The project's headquarters was at the Wright-Patterson Air Force Base near Dayton, Ohio. The project investigated a whopping 12,618 sightings, of which only 701 remained unidentified. One of the sightings they were sent to investigate in 1952 was the Flatwoods Monster. The Air Force investigators found that bright meteors had appeared in the sky at dusk, and they believed the monster spotted in the tree to be an owl.

Q: What huge cryptid is said to appear headless from behind due to its low-sitting head?

A: The Grafton Monster is a creature first sighted in West Virginia in the 1950s. The cryptid is said to weigh over one thousand pounds, have short fur, walk upright, and prey on livestock. It is also said to appear to be headless from behind due to its head resting low on its chest.

Q: What sheepish cryptid has been spotted in Point Pleasant, West Virginia?

A: This cryptid is sheepish in two senses: first, that in all but one of the reported sightings, it was said to have fled when people approached, and second, that it's part sheep! The Sheepsquatch was first reported in the 1990s when several women coming home from a family reunion were driving through the TNT area (which you can learn more about in the next entry) and saw a seven-foot-tall creature covered in white shaggy hair, with horns like a ram, a long sheep-like face, and a man's legs step out of the woods. In this and several other sightings describing a similar creature, the cryptid bolted when it saw people. But two hunters in 2013 claim that they saw a nine-foot-tall creature matching the description of Sheepsquatch, though this time, it let out a fearsome growl and ran at them. They apparently got away before it harmed them.

Q: Near what Superfund site have two cryptids been reportedly spotted?

A: There are lots of sites in the United States that are so contaminated with toxic waste and other hazardous materials that they are not safe to live or work in or near. In 1980, Congress passed the Comprehensive Environmental Response, Compensation, and Liability Act, creating what most people refer to as Superfund. Superfund gives the Environmental Protection Agency (EPA) the ability to work on decontaminating these sites. The EPA has a number of Superfund sites, and one is known as the TNT area in Point Pleasant, West Virginia. Added to Superfund in 1983, it is the former location of the US Army's West Virginia Ordnance Works, where they produced trinitrotoluene (TNT) from 1942 through 1945, and which is now littered with run-down underground bunkers and contaminated with TNT, TNT by-products, and asbestos. The site is still undergoing cleanup. In 1966 and 1967, Mothman sightings were reported in the area. And in the 1990s and after, there have been multiple sightings of Sheepsquatch (which you can read about in the previous entry).

Q: What cryptid was blamed for a dog decapitation in Maryland?

A: In late 1971, in Bowie, Maryland, in Prince George's County, the Edwards family dog Ginger went missing. That same night, sixteen-year-old Amy Edwards and some of her friends saw a strange, six-foot-tall, bipedal, hairy creature that made a high-pitched squealing sound. Days later, the poor doggie was found decapitated. The story was reported in an article in the *Prince George's County News* by Karen Hosler that mentioned the Goatman, as did a *Washington Post* article about the incident. The creature was already a local legend, having made the news in the 1950s and 1960s, but with references to him going much further back. Sometimes he's described as a half-man, half-goat creature and sometimes as a goat herder who went murderously mad after his goats were killed. Just two weeks before the sighting story, Hosler had written an article on local folklore that included the Goatman, which may have put the Goatman in people's minds before that fateful night.

Q: What government research facility was blamed for the existence of Maryland's Goatman?

A: In one version of the Maryland Goatman legend, the hybrid man-and-goat creature was the result of the experiments of a mad scientist at the Beltsville Agricultural Research Center, a very real USDA-affiliated research facility in Beltsville, Maryland, established in 1910. Modern employees of the facility have stated doubt that the Goatman came from their facility, or that the creature even exists, for that matter.

Q: What cryptid was spotted by three teens in Massachusetts in the 1970s?

A: In April 1977, over the twenty-first and twenty-second of the month, three separate teens spotted an odd creature out at night in the town of Dover, Massachusetts. Two were driving with passengers, and one was walking alone. Bill Bartlett saw it on the first night at around 10:30 p.m. He was driving and saw in his headlights an odd-looking creature perched on a stone wall on all fours, but his passengers didn't see it. A couple of hours later, John Baxter spotted a similarly odd creature while walking home. He said it was walking upright, and he called out to it thinking it was a friend, but then realized his error as he got closer. He said the thing bolted up a hill and stood against a tree. The next night, Abby Brabham was riding in a car with her boyfriend when she saw a similar creature in the headlights, crossing the road on all fours. All later had similar descriptions of the creature: hairless with peach or beige skin, a rounded head as big as its body, round glowing eyes, and four thin limbs with long fingerlike appendages at the end of them. Bartlett described these fingers gripping the stone, and Baxter described them gripping the tree trunk. Bartlett, who reportedly has a photographic memory, even drew a detailed sketch of the creature. The Dover Demon was first investigated and coined by cryptozoologist Loren Coleman. No one ever discovered what it was, and no one has seen it since, but it is still talked of to this day.

Q: What hybrid creature is said to live under a railroad bridge in Louisville, Kentucky?

A: A railroad trestle bridge that passes over Pope Lick Creek in Louisville, Kentucky, is said to be the home of a half-man and half-goat (or sometimes sheep) creature. Some even say it has wings. Called the Pope Lick Monster, it is said to lure people to their deaths on the tracks. Whether the Pope Lick Monster exists or not, he has racked up a body count. Several people have died trying to get a glimpse of the legendary monster's habitat by scaling the railway trestles.

Q: What cryptid of Northern California have hunters reported shooting right through?

A: The Ghost Deer is a very large buck said to roam in the canyons of Mount Eddy in the Trinity Mountains in Northern California. According to people who have seen the Ghost Deer, it looks more like an elk than a deer (in an area where there aren't known to be any elk), is larger than the average deer, leaves larger footprints, and has a huge rack of antlers with twelve points on one side and ten on the other. Some hunters swear they shot the deer but the bullets passed right through, and the Ghost Deer walked away unscathed.

Q: What magical amphibious cryptid was sighted in the Greater Cincinnati area?

A: In Loveland, Ohio, in May 1955, a traveling salesman traversed a bridge over the Little Miami River, and there he claimed to have spotted three frog-like creatures standing on their hind legs on the side of the road, each about three and a half feet tall, conversing with each other. As if that weren't strange enough, he said that when they noticed him sitting there watching them, one of them held up a wand and waved it at him, producing sparks. This induced the salesman to hightail it out of there. The cryptid was dubbed the Loveland Frog (sometimes also called the Loveland Frogman).

There were no similar sightings in the area until March 1972, when two separate police officers reported seeing a strange amphibious creature within two weeks of each other near the Totes boot factory and the Little Miami River. The first saw a three- to four-foot-tall frog-like creature run across the road in front of his car and jump the guardrail into the river. The second officer saw a lump in the road close to the first sighting. When he went to remove what he thought was roadkill, the creature jumped at him and ran under the guardrail. The officer shot and killed the creature. Upon inspection, it turned out to be an iguana with a missing tail.

In August 2016, two Pokémon Go players also reportedly spotted what looked to them like a giant frog near Lake Isabella in Loveland. They posted photos and video, although it was dark and the images mostly show glowing eyes.

Q: What smelly cryptid is said to inhabit the swamps of Florida?

A: The Skunk Ape is a cryptid that is said to inhabit the swamplands of the Florida Everglades. The creature is described as being a hominid akin to Bigfoot, standing anywhere from five to seven feet tall, covered in dark or red hair, with (according to reported footprint evidence) four toes on each foot. The creature is said to have been part of Florida folklore for decades, but most sightings have been recorded since the 1970s.

The thing that differentiates Skunk Ape sightings the most from typical Bigfoot sightings is the description of the foul stench that emanates from the creatures. Skunk Apes are said to reek of methane, manure, rotten eggs, decaying garbage, or, as one might expect, skunks.

Q: What white, hairy cryptid is reported to roam several counties in Alabama?

A: Sightings of the Alabama White Thang ("thing" with a Southern twang) have been reported since the 1940s in and around the counties of Etowah, Jefferson, and Morgan in the state of Alabama, including several sightings in the Wheeler National Wildlife Refuge. Eyewitnesses have described a white, hairy creature standing eight feet tall (although sometimes also spotted on four legs), with glowing red eyes. Some describe the Alabama White Thang as looking like a big cat and some like a hybrid creature with a kangaroo-like body and a catlike head. It is also said to be able to move swiftly and to emit a terrifying high-pitched scream.

Q: The sighting of what large reptile resulted in a hunt in Churubusco, Indiana, in 1949?

A: The Beast of 'Busco is named for the town where it reportedly resided, Churubusco, Indiana, about ten miles northwest of Fort Wayne. The "beast," more affectionately known as Oscar, was thought to live in and around Fulk Lake. Although possibly first sighted as early as 1900, a 1949 sighting garnered media attention, and hundreds of people flocked to the town to witness a publicized hunt for the beast that ran for two months. Even with trappers, pilots, divers, and a draining of the lake, the search was unsuccessful. And unlike many reported lake monsters, this one has a very recognizable description: a snapping turtle! But at a reported four feet across, Oscar was an unusually large snapping turtle, thus his beastly moniker.

Q: What three-legged beast reportedly spotted in Illinois was thought by some to be a space alien?

A: The Enfield Horror, sometimes called the Enfield Monster, was described by its main eyewitness in the small village of Enfield, Illinois, as a four-and-a-half-foot-tall gray creature with large pink eyes, two arms, and three legs ending in six-toed feet with which it could jump long distances. The beast was first sighted by Henry McDaniel the night of April 25, 1973. He said something scratched at his door, and he thought he saw a bear outside, so he went outside with a flashlight and a gun and saw the terrifying three-legged creature in his garden. He shot the creature, which he said hissed at him and bounded away, reaching fifty feet in only three leaps. McDaniel believed the creature to be an alien from outer space. McDaniel told a local radio station he saw it again walking the railroad tracks near his house, and they sent out a news crew who reported seeing an apelike creature in the area. People went looking for it, including a party of men who were charged with hunting violations for drinking and reportedly firing on the creature. A 1978 paper cited social contagion (sometimes also called "sociogenic illness" or "mass hysteria") as the probable cause of multiple sightings of the creature, and that eyewitnesses may have instead been seeing multiple real animals.

Q: What cryptid reportedly surfaced when a sinkhole was flooded?

A: To the southeast of Inman, Kansas, in an area known as Section 27, there is a sinkhole aptly and officially named Big Sinkhole that eventually filled with water. In 1952, Albert Neufeld, an eighteen-year-old Mennonite, saw a long snake or wormlike creature in the waters of the sinkhole and fired two shots at it. There have been several sightings since then of Sinkhole Sam, described as anywhere from fifteen to thirty feet long and as big around as a tire. Some have also added that it has a fin down its back, a grooved tail, and what looks like a grin on its face.

In 1953, a satirist for the *Salina Journal* wrote a parody article calling the creature a "foopengerkle," which brought cryptid hunters to the area despite the article's tongue-in-cheek nature. Mary Kay Flynn of the Newspaper Enterprise Association wrote a more serious article in 1953 after interviewing eyewitnesses. And thus the legend of Sinkhole Sam was born.

Q: What ghostly hooved creature is said to haunt the woods of Maine?

A: While probably not an actual ghost, there were a few sightings in Maine of an ethereal white moose with a ten-foot-wide rack of antlers that stands up to fifteen feet high starting at the end of the nineteenth century. The first sighting was reported in the *New York Times* in 1899, where a man said he saw an all-white moose near Lobster Lake in northern Maine. Other sightings popped up from 1901 to 1932. The Specter Moose is not to be confused with Ghost Moose, which are moose suffering from a pitiable condition caused by thousands of tick bites.

Q: What hybrid Michigan creature reportedly appears every ten years?

A: The Michigan Dogman was a cryptid first seen in 1887 by two loggers who said they chased what they thought was a dog into a corner. One of the men reportedly poked the creature with a stick, prompting it to stand upright and reveal its human body, and making the lumberjacks hightail it out of there. The cryptid is described as standing seven feet tall, with either yellow or blue eyes, a dog's head, and a human body. It reportedly emits a frightening humanlike howl. The Dogman is said to appear every ten years, always in a year ending in the number seven.

Q: What terrorized two fishermen on the Pascagoula River in Mississippi?

A: Two men fishing at night on the Pascagoula River in Mississippi claimed they heard a zipping sound and then saw a glowing craft shaped like an egg floating above the ground.

According to the fishermen, three five-foot-tall robot-like aliens emerged, abducted the men, and performed experiments on them. These extraterrestrials became known as the Pascagoula River Aliens.

Q: For what hairy quadrupedal cryptid does a body exist that the owners refuse to allow to be tested?

A: The Shunka Warak'in (which apparently means "carries off dogs" in the language of the Iowa First Nations people) is a beast that terrorized Montanans in the 1880s. It reportedly looked somewhat like a wolf, but with higher shoulders and a back that sloped downward somewhat like a hyena's, and very dark hair. A rancher shot the creature and reportedly gave it to an Idahoan grocer who had it stuffed and displayed it under the name "ringdocus." According to one report, the current owner won't allow the remains to be genetically tested to confirm what it really was.

Q: What large aquatic reptile is said to inhabit a lake near the Sandhills of Nebraska?

A: Walgren Lake (which used to be called Alkali Lake) is located in northwestern Nebraska near the Sandhills. Aside from good fishing, the lake is known for its own lake monster: the Alkali Lake Monster (also known as the Walgren Lake Monster). Originating from local First Nations legends of a horned serpent in the waters, the Alkali Lake Monster is described as a brown, forty- to one-hundred-foot-long alligator-like creature with a horn on its nose and a terrible odor. The first newspaper reports occurred in the early 1920s. Residents have since blamed the creature for pet disappearances, but it is thought that these reports were the work of Nebraska newspaperman and known hoaxer John G. Maher, who, aside from publicizing the monster, also created fake soda springs near Chadron, Nebraska, using sacks of soda, and wrote of the so-called discovery of a preserved prehistoric man in the same area.

Q: What New Hampshire cryptid is said to be able to blend in with the woods to an eerie degree?

A: The Wood Devils are described as skinny, bipedal, seven-foot-tall creatures covered in gray hair with long, pointy faces and sharp teeth. Sightings began in the early 1900s, with most occurring from the 1930s to the 1970s. The creatures are said to inhabit the woods of Coös County in New Hampshire near its border with Canada. The Wood Devils are also known for their ability to blend in seamlessly with the surrounding woods by either hiding or standing completely still to camouflage themselves among the trees. They are also said to avoid humans and to bolt away at great speed when people get too close.

Q: What cryptid terrorized residents of a North Carolina town in 1953 and 2003?

A: In December 1953 near Bladenboro, North Carolina, sightings of a big cat coincided with a spate of attacks on pets and livestock. The animals were exsanguinated (drained of blood), and their jaws were mutilated or missing. The creature even reportedly pounced at a local woman (Mrs. C. E. Kinslaw) but ran away when she screamed. The feline was dubbed the Beast of Bladenboro. Hunters were unsuccessful at finding and eradicating the creature, but it disappeared on its own. However, a similar spate of animal mutilations was reported in Bladenboro in 2003—exactly fifty years later.

Q: What Pennsylvania cryptid is said to be able to dissolve into a puddle of tears?

A: The Squonk is said to inhabit the hemlock groves of Pennsylvania and is described as a piglike creature with loose, wrinkly skin that is covered in warts and moles. William Thomas Cox, in his fanciful 1910 book *Fearsome Creatures of the Lumberwoods, With a Few Desert and Mountain Beasts*, wrote of the Squonk, "Probably the homeliest animal in the world, and knows it." The poor Squonk ostensibly sheds tears constantly because it knows how unattractive it is, and it can reportedly dissolve into a puddle of tears to escape capture.

Q: What "vampire" reportedly killed most of her family in the late 1800s in Rhode Island?

A: In 1883 in Exeter, Rhode Island, George Brown, a local farmer, began losing family members. His wife, Mary, died that year, followed by their daughter Mary Olive (twenty years old) a few months later. In 1892, their teenage daughter Mercy passed away, and their teenage son Edwin became ill. The likely actual cause of the downfall of most of the family was diagnosed by the town doctor: tuberculosis (known then as "consumption"). But some of the townsfolk believed that a vampire was to blame. They dug up the bodies of the deceased Brown family (Mary, Mary Olive, and recently deceased Mercy) and discovered in horror that Mercy's body had not decomposed in two months (likely because it was the dead of winter and the body was frozen). This led them to remove and burn her heart so that she would no longer suck the life from the living. They also added some of the ashes to medicine for Edwin, but he died of his illness a few weeks later. Mercy and other suspected vampires in Rhode Island in the late-nineteenth century led to Rhode Island being considered the vampire capital of America for a time.

Q: **What large, lizard-like creature terrorized Lee County, South Carolina, locals in 1988?**

A: On June 29, 1988, sightings of a seven-foot-tall, green, scaly, lizard-like monster with red eyes and three fingers on each hand occurred in the swamplands of Lee County, South Carolina. The first report was made by seventeen-year-old Christopher Davis, who stopped to fix a flat near the Scape Ore Swamp on his way home from work at 2:00 a.m. He heard a noise behind him and turned to see what is now known as the Lizard Man of Scape Ore Swamp (aka the Lizard Man of Lee County) racing toward him. He jumped in his car and sped off, but the creature climbed on his roof and tried to get in until the kid shook him off. The car had scratches on the roof and a broken side-view mirror. Other reports came in over the next month of sightings of the creature, who was said to roam the swamps and the subway and sewer systems in nearby towns. Radio station WCOS offered a million-dollar reward to anyone who could bring in the animal alive, but it remained unclaimed.

Q: **What is South Dakota's Bigfoot-like cryptid called?**

A: South Dakota's (and possibly Northern Nebraska's) Taku-He is described as a tall, hairy bipedal creature with long arms rather like Bigfoot. But unlike Bigfoot, it seems to have a penchant for mutilating livestock and wildlife genitalia—and is sometimes depicted as donning a top hat! Sightings of a Bigfoot-like creature began in 1974 in Pierce County, Nebraska (where a cow was mutilated and exsanguinated), and Jefferson, South Dakota (where someone saw a large bipedal creature dragging its own furry prey across a field). In 1977, dozens of similar sightings (but sans the mutilations) were reported in and around Little Eagle, South Dakota, in the Standing Rock Indian Reservation, home of Dakota and Lakota Sioux First Nations peoples. No one claimed that the shaggy creature was wearing a top hat, but read on to find out about another entity that may be conflated with the Bigfoot-like Taku-He by cryptozoologists that has led to images of a stovepipe hat–wearing Sasquatch.

Q: What horrifying South Dakota cryptid is said to wear a stovepipe hat?

A: Like the Bigfoot creature from the previous entry, this entity is sometimes referred to as Taku-He, but he also goes by the name Walking Sam or Tall Man. He is described as a seven- to ten-foot-tall slim man wearing a stovepipe hat, and he is alternately described as having no face, or having eyes but no mouth. This spirit is said to whisper to young people and convince them to kill themselves. Mainly reported in Pine Ridge, South Dakota (an Oglala Lakota tribal area), there have been recurring reports of Walking Sam in the 1980s and in 2007, and more recently, from December 2014 to March 2015, during which time 103 people under the age of twenty-five attempted suicide, and, sadly, nine succeeded. Walking Sam is a legend that embodies a crisis that is all too real.

Q: What large amphibian has reportedly been spotted in the Trinity Alps Wilderness in California?

A: Sightings of larger-than-expected salamanders have been reported in the Trinity Alps Wilderness area in northern California since the 1920s, when hunter Frank L. Griffith reported seeing in a lake five salamanders that measured from five to nine feet long each. Salamanders around the lower end of that range do exist, the largest being the Chinese giant salamander (*Andrias davidianus*), which can reach up to six feet in length, though none that large are known to inhabit North America. The largest known salamander in the US is the hellbender (*Cryptobranchus alleganiensis*), a creature whose name sounds like it should be that of a cryptid, or even a demon, but it is just a giant salamander that reaches up to twenty-nine inches in length and inhabits the waters of Appalachia and areas in Arkansas, Indiana, Illinois, Kentucky, Missouri, and Ohio. The fact that nobody has been able to capture or otherwise document the existence of these oversized Trinity Alps salamanders makes them cryptids. The fact that most salamanders don't have gills or lungs and breathe by absorbing oxygen through their skin—that just makes them cool.

Q: What monster is said to inhabit a lake island in Texas?

A: Greer Island is a landmass in the middle of Lake Worth, a body of water at the edge of the city of Lake Worth, Texas, east of Fort Worth. The island is said to be the home of the Lake Worth Monster, a seven-foot-tall, half-goat half-man creature said to be covered in fur and, oddly, also in scales. The beast reportedly jumped on someone's car and was only thrown when the driver hit a tree. In 1969, Allen Plaster took a photo of the creature, but he stated in more recent years that he believes it to have been a hoax.

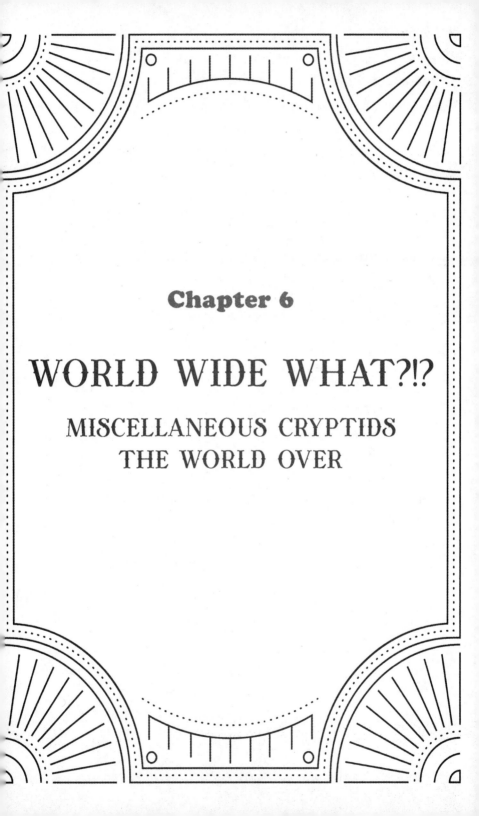

Chapter 6

WORLD WIDE WHAT?!?

MISCELLANEOUS CRYPTIDS
THE WORLD OVER

Q: What cryptid is depicted on the grave of a woman reportedly killed by the creature?

A: The Dobhar-chú is a seven-foot-long, half-hound, half-fish, otter-like lake creature of Irish lore that can travel via water or land and eats people. Its name means something like "water hound," and it is sometimes also called the Irish Crocodile. In 1722 in the town of Creevelea, Glenade, County Leitrim in Ireland, Grace McGloighlin (aka Grace Connolly) reportedly went down to the lake and was killed by a huge monster, which her husband found asleep atop her dead body. On her grave in Conwall Cemetery is carved an image of the beast that killed her, replete with a spear through the beast that reportedly killed it!

Q: What Hawaiian mythical, or not so mythical, men are known for showing up to build amazing structures overnight?

A: The Menehune of Hawaii are described as small men anywhere from six inches to two feet tall who appear in the night and build things like temples, roads, canoes, and fishponds—and to complete their projects in one night! They are said to cease all work if anyone sees them. Several famous, well-crafted, and advanced architectural marvels are attributed to them. These structures were already present when people from Tahiti arrived around 1100 CE and colonized the islands, and they include the Alekoko fishpond (made with stones from twenty-five miles away) and the wall of the Kikiaola Ditch, both in Kauai, as well as the ceremonial stones (heiau) on Necker Island. See Chapter Seven for a plausible explanation of who these "small" people might have been.

Q: What beast did King Louis XV of France reportedly send troops to kill?

A: In June 1764, a large wolflike beast apparently began attacking and often killing people in the mountainous area of Gévaudan in the southeast of France, an area now called Lozère. Dubbed the Beast of Gévaudan, it was said to be responsible for the killings of more than seventy people from 1764 to 1767. Eyewitnesses described the beast as taller than a wolf, with reddish fur with dark stripes, a large head with a long snout full of sharp teeth, and short, pointy ears. Some also said that it appeared impervious to bullets, could leap great distances, and could stand on its back legs. It was thought by some to be a *loup-garou* (werewolf in French). King Louis XV sent the cavalry to fell the beast, which apparently saw and fired upon it, but to no avail. A renowned wolf hunter named Denneval also failed to slay the beast. Over a few years, several wolves were killed as the possible culprits. But in June 1767, a party was sent by the Marquis d'Apcher to hunt the beast, and one member, Jean Chastel, killed a creature that more closely fit the description than the wolves. In the 1990s, a taxidermist researched the archives of the National Museum of Natural History and discovered that a specimen similar to the slain Beast of Gévaudan had been on display at the museum until 1819, and it was identified as a hyena.

Q: What half felid creature is said to drive people insane?

A: The Wampus cat is an Appalachian cryptid whose glance is sometimes said to drive people insane. The creature is always described as feline, but sometimes also as half dog or half woman. The Wampus cat likely derived from the Cherokee legend of Ew-Ah and Running Deer. In one telling, Running Deer's husband was sent to slay the demon Ew-Ah who was terrorizing the village, but he returned a madman. Running Deer wanted revenge, so she donned a bobcat mask given to her by the shamans, snuck up on Ew-Ah, and seeing the spirit of the mountain cat, Ew-Ah himself went insane. The spirit of Running Deer is said to still roam the forest as a protector.

Q: What mysterious foe did the First Duke of Wellington go out on horseback to hunt?

A: In 1838 in London, a man or manlike creature was reported jumping from rooftop to rooftop and attacking women all over the city. He was described by one victim as wearing a tight white costume and a helmet, and spitting blue and white flames. Others added that he had fiery eyes and cold clawlike fingers. The police investigated the sightings and attacks, and Arthur Wellesley, the 1st Duke of Wellington, who was sixty-nine at the time, went out on horseback with the aim of finding and killing the beast, who was dubbed Spring-heeled Jack. He continued to pop up all over England over the next few decades. He was even reported to have jumped on an army sentry box, scaring the soldiers posted there and prompting the army to set traps for him. The last Spring-heeled Jack sighting was in 1904 in Liverpool. To this day, no one knows who he was.

Q: What flora in South and Central America is said to kill humans and other animals?

A: Not all cryptids are animals, which is where cryptobotany comes in. Starting with the book Sea and Land by J. W. Buel, published in 1887, accounts of the Ya-Te-Veo, a man-eating tree said to inhabit South and Central America, began to appear. The tree is described as having moving tentacle-like branches that grab its victims (from small animals to horses) and swallow them into its thick trunk. Some even depict the tree with eyes.

Q: What cryptid is said to protect the Amazon rainforest?

A: The Mapinguari is a creature of Indigenous folklore that is said to not only inhabit the Amazon rainforest but to protect it. Tales of the creature appeared around the turn of the twentieth century. The Mapinguari is said to be a large, hairy, cave-dwelling creature around seven feet tall with a short snout on its face; a large, vertical mouth full of sharp teeth in the middle of its abdominal cavity; and long, hooked claws on all four paws, which are sometimes said to be turned backwards. Some describe it as having two eyes, but some say that the Mapinguari has a single eye in the center of its forehead. The creature is reported to alternate between walking upright and walking on all fours. It is known to emit a particularly foul odor and to possibly have the power to disorient its prey. The creature is said to be mostly impervious to weapons, but that its weak spot is its navel. No one is certain, but the name Mapinguari is thought to come from the language of the Tupi Guarani people and to mean "thing with twisted feet." The Mapinguari is said to devour people who try to harm the forest and its creatures.

Q: What wily reptile is said to be able to curl up and roll after its prey?

A: The hoop snake has been reported since the colonization of North America by Europeans. The creature is described as a snake with the ability to stick its tail in its mouth, roll after its victims, and sting with its venomous tail stinger. Reputed ways to escape are to run behind a tree as it strikes or to jump a fence to make it uncurl. As far as science is concerned, they don't exist. But see Chapter Seven, "Skeptical Analysis: Possible Scientific Explanations," for one possible inspiration for tales of the hoop snake.

Q: What cryptid is said to deal out death in the Gobi desert?

A: The Mongolian deathworm, know to locals as allghoi khorkhoi (or "intestine worm") is described as a blood-red, two-foot to five-foot-long worm the thickness of a person's arm and the shape of a sausage. This deathworm is said to possess the threats of electrocuting people from a distance, being deadly poisonous to touch, and spitting an acid-like venom, which is said to burn through skin, enter the bloodstream, and turn its victims yellow.

Q: What creature of Algonquian lore was said to have once been a human hunter?

A: The Wendigo (or Windigo) is a cryptid that is said to inhabit the forests of Canada and the northernmost portions of North America and is part of Plains and First Nations folklore. The beast is described as a tall (sometimes as much as fifteen feet tall), emaciated creature with long arms and legs, ash-gray skin, and sometimes sharp claws and large glowing eyes, with a taste for human flesh. The Wendigo is said to be able to mimic people's voices and to use the capability to lure people and devour them. The creature is also said to be able to possess people and cause them to crave human flesh, as well. In Algonquian folklore, the Wendigo began life as a hunter who became lost one winter and turned to cannibalism rather than starve. This horrific act turned him into a monster. Most Wendigo sightings occurred from the 1800s to the 1920s, and some anthropologists argue that the concept of the Wendigo didn't appear until after First Nations peoples encountered Europeans and their brutality.

Q: What mysterious specters are said to watch over the mountains of the Central California coast?

A: The Santa Lucia Range in California is reportedly home to entities called the Dark Watchers, or *Los Vigilantes Oscuros* by Spanish colonizers, or the Old Ones by the Chumash First Nations people who inhabited the Central California coast for centuries. They are reported as dark humanoid silhouettes seven to fifteen feet tall, wearing wide-brimmed hats and dark capes or cloaks, and sometimes carrying staffs. Eyewitnesses don't report seeing their faces, and they reportedly disappear when people try to approach them. They are said usually to appear at dusk or dawn, but some sightings have been in the afternoon, as well. And most say the Dark Watcher or Watchers stand silent and still, seemingly looking over the landscape, although one eyewitness said he waved, and the watcher waved back!

Q: What Tanzanian cryptid was mentioned in the British scientific journal *Discover* in the late 1930s?

A: The Mngwa, which is from the Swahili word *mungwa* that translates to "the strange one," is said to be a humongous gray feline roughly the size of a donkey with small ears and stripes that resemble those of a human-friendly tabby cat. It is also sometimes called a Nunda, which can mean "fierce animal." But this less-than-human-friendly cat is said to have mauled several police officers in 1922 in Lindi, Tanzania, and several more in the 1930s in Mchinga, Tanzania. William Hichens wrote of the Nunda (Mngwa) in a 1937 article in *Discover* called "African Mystery Beasts." Reported in Tanzania for hundreds of years, some believe it is a cat species that survived from the Pleistocene era. Naturalist Frank W. Lane in his 1954 book *Nature Parade* suggested attacks in South Africa by another cryptid, the Nandi bear, or chimiset or chemosit, might have been Mngwa attacks. See Chapter Seven for a scientifically classified and currently living animal that might be related to the elusive Mngwa.

Q: What "bear" is reportedly encountered on a continent that has no bear species confirmed to live there?

A: The chimisit (which goes by a number of other regional names) is often called the Nandi bear after the Nandi people of western Kenya. The Nandi bear is often described as a half-bear, half-hyena cryptid with reported sightings in various parts of the continent of Africa. But as far as science is concerned, there are no members of the family *Ursidae,* to which bears belong, in Africa.

Q: What legendary Brazilian creature is said to sometimes redirect waterways?

A: The Minhocão is a purported giant armored earthworm or snake said to measure as much as fifty yards long and five yards wide, and to dwell most of its life underground but occasionally surface and uproot trees, displace earth, and leave wide trenches that sometimes divert waterways. Reportedly Indigenous to Brazil, an article "A New Underground Monster" in the February 21, 1878, issue of *Nature* gave details of several reported sightings, along with occasions where people saw or felt signs that a Minhocão had been present (the earth shaking or land destroyed with telltale trenches), spanning the mid to late 1800s.

Q: What cryptid is described by what it is not rather than what it is?

A: The Not Deer is a cryptid that is reported to look a lot like a deer, but with some features that are decidedly *not* like a deer. For instance, sightings of the Not Deer report it having limbs that aren't the same length as a deer and that do not move as you'd expect a deer's limbs to move, and eyes that are either too close together or forward facing (more like a predator's than a prey animal's eyes). According to JD Sword of the *Skeptical Inquirer*, Not Deer reports began appearing on Tumblr and Reddit in 2019 and TikTok in 2020, with an earlier 4Chan post describing an odd deerlike creature that fit the description of the Not Deer but not calling it that. Not Deer sightings are most often in Appalachia.

Q: What cryptid was first sighted in Puerto Rico in the 1990s?

A: In 1995, near Morovis and Orocovis in Puerto Rico, chickens, goats, and other animals were found slaughtered and apparently drained of blood. Shortly thereafter, sightings began. The creature has been described as having red eyes with no eyelids, a round head, sharp fangs, short fur, spikes running down its back, wiry arms with clawed hands, large muscular back legs, and occasionally wings. Due to its penchant for goat blood, the creature was dubbed the Chupacabra, meaning "goat sucker." Since then, sightings have been reported in other parts of the US and in Mexico.

Q: What mythical creature terrorized a Serbian village in 2012?

A: In the small Serbian village of Zorazje, an old watermill by the Rogačica River is thought to be the stomping grounds of Sava Savanovic, who sold flour from the mill in the 1700s. It is said that, one day, villagers found him dead with two puncture wounds on his neck, and that a yellow butterfly flew from his mouth. Afterward, he was believed to haunt the area as a vampire who would desanguinate and kill villagers who came to grind their grain at the mill. For decades, the mill sat mostly unused and unrepaired because the owners were afraid to do anything that might disturb and awaken Savanovic. In 2012, due to the lack of repair, the watermill collapsed. The villagers feared this meant that Savanovic was loose in the woods and looking for a new home—and new victims to drain of their blood. People in the area hung crosses over their doors and bought lots of garlic for protection. And the town council even put out a public health warning about the potential vampire threat.

Q: What striped cryptid reportedly roams East Australia's Queensland region?

A: The Queensland Tiger, aka yarri, is a cryptid with sightings that go back centuries in Aboriginal circles. It was first reported by outsiders in 1871, and there was a spate of sightings south of the tropical rainforest of North Queensland in the 1940s and '50s. This creature is described as feline with long, sharp teeth; sharp claws; tan fur; dark stripes all over its body; and a long, striped tail. The Queensland Tiger is said to measure about the size of a large dog.

Q: What man-eating mythical creature is said to roam the billabongs of Australia?

A: In Aboriginal Australian mythology, the Bunyip is a large creature said to live in billabongs (bodies of water leftover from flooding) and occasionally attack and eat people. Their description varies widely, sometimes as seal-like, sometimes emu-like, anywhere from dog to horse size, with a round head and long neck, sometimes quadrupedal, with variations of horns, fur, scales, fangs, or tusks, and the body of anything from a manatee to an ox, or sometimes even a human. It is also said to unleash a terrifying cry.

Q: What big cat is said to roam the moors of Somerset and Devon in the United Kingdom?

A: The Beast of Exmoor is a large feline cryptid said to roam an area in the United Kingdom known as Exmoor (moorlands that cover west Somerset and north Devon). Sightings have been reported since the 1970s of a large cat up to eight feet long, with either black, brown, tan, or gray hair. The creature has been blamed for livestock killings, including from a farmer who found over one hundred of his sheep slaughtered within three months of each other in 1983. After that incident, the Royal Marines were sent to the area to kill the Beast of Exmoor, and although they reportedly glimpsed at least one large feline, it proved wily and elusive, and no one was able to shoot it.

Q: What beast reportedly stalks the moors of Cornwall, England?

A: In the 1990s, people in the Cornwall area, a county in southwestern England, began to report slain livestock and sightings of big cats akin to leopards in the area, especially around Bodmin Moor. The sightings led the supposed feline creatures to be called the Beast of Bodmin Moor. In 1995, the Ministry of Agriculture, Fisheries, and Food conducted an official investigation and found no evidence of large cats roaming the area, although sightings continue, including of purported paw prints.

Q: What creature is said to appear and sodomize men who don't believe in him?

A: Popobawa is a sort of dwarfish incubus with one eye, sharp talons, pointy ears, and bat wings who is said to appear in a puff of smoke in bedrooms on the Pemba and Zanzibar islands of Tanzania and rape men who don't believe he exists. Popobawa means "bat wing" in the Swahili language. There have been many reports of the creature appearing, especially in times of societal stress. Fear of Popobawa has even prompted some men to sleep in groups outside. Like the incubus, some reports are believed to be the result of sleep paralysis (which can cause the feeling of being held down and hallucination, among other symptoms). And mass hysteria might account for the increase of sightings that sometimes occur at certain times.

Q: What man-eating plant was said to inhabit an area that is now in southern Egypt and northern Sudan?

A: In 1881, a man named Phil Robinson collected stories from his uncle into a book. The uncle had apparently explored Nubia, an area that now straddles southern Egypt and northern Sudan. One of the stories from his uncle was of the Nubian Tree, which according to him has flowers with an attractive scent and fruit the color of honey with which it lured unsuspecting animals, including people, to their deaths. The tree would apparently grab its prey with its branches and devour them. Stories from a nineteenth-century colonial explorer to his nephew should perhaps be taken with a grain of salt or two.

Q: What killer vine was reported in British magazines in the 1890s?

A: Around 1892, accounts began circulating in British magazines of a killer vine encountered by a naturalist named Mr. Dunstan (no first name given). Dunstan was said to have been exploring the flora of Nicaragua when he heard his dog cry out in pain, and when he found him, the dog was reportedly surrounded by branch-like vines that exuded an adhesive resin. He freed the dog and found that he was covered in bloody spots where the vine had apparently sucked his blood. Dunstan said it grabbed and left marks on his hands, as well. He reported that it seemed to suck the blood from animals and drop the flesh, and that he spoke to locals who called it "the Devil's Snare." This botanical cryptid, which seems to exist only in this one report, is also often referred to as "the Vampire Vine," likely due to its purported blood sucking.

Q: What mammalian creature has been sighted in a country that has no Indigenous land mammals?

A: The Waitoreke is a creature thought by some to inhabit New Zealand, described as around two feet long with short limbs, brown fur, and a bushy tail, kind of like an otter or beaver, with an affinity for water. The creature was reportedly first seen in 1773, with other sightings occurring up through the 1970s. However, the country of New Zealand has no Indigenous land mammals except for a couple of varieties of bat. The Waitoreke is considered a creature of folklore. It is possible that eyewitnesses were seeing some other animal introduced by outsiders to New Zealand or were just mistaking seals or other aquatic mammals for land mammals.

Q: What cryptid is a sometimes a foe but sometimes a friend to miners?

A: The Tommyknockers began as a superstition from miners in Cornwall, England. They were supposedly two-foot-tall men in mining outfits who did a mix of mischief and good in the mines, sometimes saving miners and sometimes harming them. The knocking noises that occur just before mine collapses were sometimes attributed to them. During the California Gold Rush in the United States, Cornish miners came to the US, and the legend of the Tommyknockers came with them. At some point, they morphed from little people into the ghosts of dead miners. In either case, miners in the US would sometimes leave these ghostly cryptids offerings in hopes of gaining their favor and not meeting bad luck in the dangerous mines. And occasionally mines where lots of bad things happened would have to be shut down because of miners' fear of the Tommyknockers (or perhaps of the poor mining conditions). These spirits are said to have moved on to haunting the homes near old mines, where they warn of bad things coming by knocking on the walls.

Q: What reptilian cryptid is said to have roamed in the valleys of the Himalayas?

A: The Yeti isn't the only cryptid reported in the Himalayas. The Buru is said to have been a twenty-foot-long aquatic creature akin to a monitor lizard (like a Komodo dragon) that inhabited the Himalayan valleys of Assam, India. But alas, even cryptozoologists believe this valley cryptid to have gone extinct, at least in that region. Another twenty-foot-long aquatic lizard referred to as the jhoor has been reported in other parts of India, and similar large lizards have been reported in Bhutan and Bangladesh.

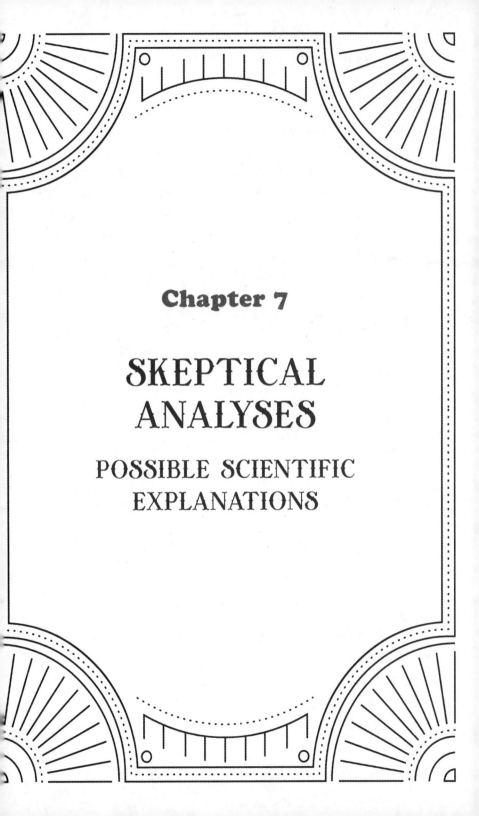

Chapter 7

SKEPTICAL ANALYSES

POSSIBLE SCIENTIFIC EXPLANATIONS

Q: What real-life goliaths were likely responsible for Kraken sightings?

A: The Norwegian mythological beast the Kraken is said to destroy whole ships and their crews. But there is likely a real animal behind early belief in this creature. The giant squid, scientific name *Architeuthis dux,* is a cephalopod that has a beak and tentacles with pointy toothlike objects on its tentacle suckers. It can reach nearly sixty feet in length. It's no wonder sailors imagined the worst when they saw it. The giant squid was officially classified by Norwegian scientist Japetus Steenstrup after a specimen washed up on a beach in Denmark in 1853.

Aside from the obvious similarities to the giant squid, some of the precursors to the emergence of a Kraken described by sailors, like bubbles, fish rising to the surface, extreme currents, and new land formations, can be caused by volcanic activity underwater. Perhaps some Icelandic eruptions were mistakenly attributed to the beast.

Q: What fossil evidence has led some to suspect there really was a Kraken-sized cephalopod at some point?

A: Ichthyosaurs were forty-five-foot-long marine dinosaurs that are believed to have existed from around 250 million to 90 million years ago (through the Triassic, Jurassic, and Cretaceous periods of the Mesozoic era). At a dig site in Nevada, the twisted and broken bones of nine 220-million-year-old Shonisaurus ichthyosaurs were found arranged in a geometric pattern that seemed unlikely to have been caused by natural phenomena such as currents. Paleontologist Mark McMenamin has hypothesized that the bones may have been a midden pile (a trash heap that often includes discarded bones or shells) arranged by an unknown giant octopus large enough to have preyed upon the dinosaurs, and which he has dubbed a Triassic Kraken.

Q: **What one-horned extinct animal could possibly account for the unicorns of myth?**

A: *Elasmotherium sibiricum* was a large rhinoceros-like herbivore with thick fur and a long, single horn atop its head. For this reason, it is also referred to as the Siberian unicorn. The *Elasmotherium* was originally thought to have gone extinct over 100,000 years ago, but more recent fossil discoveries have revealed that the creatures survived much longer than originally thought, at least until 39,000 years ago and maybe even as recently as 35,000 years ago. We now know that it roamed the earth with modern humankind, and stories of these very real (at the time) creatures could have been passed down through the generations and become the unicorns of lore.

Q: **What might account for Hawaiian tales of tiny men who built great works in the night?**

A: Some historians and archeologists believe that the Menehune (see Chapter Six) were a real people who inhabited the Hawaiian Islands long before the Polynesian people arrived, possibly descendants of the Marquesas people who lived on the islands from around 0 to 350 CE. The Menehune's name may have come from Manahune, meaning something like "lowly people," or people without mana (power), and this may have led to the idea in later legends that the Menehune were small in stature (rather than in status). And they may not have truly disappeared. In a census in 1820, sixty-five people identified themselves as Menehune.

Q: What animal may account for many Chupacabra sightings?

A: Chupacabras were first reportedly sighted in 1995 in Puerto Rico, but since then have been reported all over North America. Many of these sightings are believed to be diseased coyotes, particularly coyotes with mange, a skin condition caused by parasitic mites burrowing into the skin or hair follicles of their victims. Symptoms can include hair loss and thickened, scabby, or flaky skin, which could account for making the animals less recognizable. In fact, a rancher in Cuero, Texas, Phylis Canion, found a dead blue-gray creature on the road that she suspected was one of several she had spotted on the property that were responsible for killing her chickens. She saved the head of the apparent Chupacabra for genetic analysis. It turned out to be the hybrid progeny of a coyote and a wolf that was afflicted with mange.

Q: What encounters do some scholars think may have contributed the Basajaun to Basque mythology?

A: Some people believe that the shaggy-haired Basajaun of Basque mythology (see Chapter Two for a full description) might have its roots in encounters the predecessors to the Basque people had with the Neanderthals, who lived alongside *Homo sapiens* in the area for around 10,000 years until the Neanderthals died out around 40,000 years ago. In fact, the Pyrenees was among the last areas where Neanderthals lived. And apparently, they were more advanced in toolmaking than their *Homo sapiens* cousins at the time, lending some credence to the hypothesis.

Q: What did Chinese apothecaries sell as "dragon's teeth"?

A: Paleontologists used to visit the drugstores of China in search of fossils. In fact, the first specimens of the ancient, extinct giant ape *Gigantophithecus blacki* were bought by German Dutch paleontologist G. H. R. von Koenigswald in the 1930s. They were sold as "dragon's teeth."

Q: What real birds might account for thunderbird sightings?

A: In the 1940s, there was a spate of sightings of huge birds around Alton, Illinois, which also happens to be home of an old Cahokia nation cliff drawing of a thunderbird called the Piasa Bird (a nation that formerly inhabited what became Illinois but was forcefully relocated like so many other Indigenous peoples). And the most famous purported thunderbird sighting was in 1977 in Lawndale, Illinois, when Ruth Lowe saw two huge birds with what she said were ten-foot wingspans attacking her ten-year-old son. They apparently carried him thirty-five feet with her chasing them before they dropped the child. The police didn't believe the family, and neighbors ostracized them, some even throwing dead birds onto the Lowes' yard after the incident. Two birds are often mentioned as possible stand-ins for the huge avian cryptid. One that fits the bill, so to speak, is the California condor, which has a wingspan of up to ten feet, dark feathers over its body, and a light head coloring. It is the largest known bird in North America, where the thunderbird is said to haunt the skies. But it usually keeps to the West Coast. A more likely culprit for sightings in Illinois is the turkey vulture, which has dark feathers, a red head, and an average wingspan of six feet. Six feet is far shy of ten, and definitely shy of seventy, but one might be forgiven for not accurately judging a bird's wingspan when under attack.

Q: What winged New Mexico cryptid once existed?

A: Teratorns are described as huge birds with bald, pinkish heads; black bodies; and a wingspan of up to twenty feet. These cryptids are said to appear in the skies over the state of New Mexico.

But teratorns were real creatures of the Pleistocene era. There is evidence of more than one variety of this huge ancient bird. The two whose fossils were found in North America are *Teratornis merriami* (which had 11.5- to 13.1-foot wingspans) and *Ailornis incredibilis* (which had 16.4- to 18-foot wingspans). Another found in Argentina (*Argentavis magnificens*) had a massive wingspan of 19.7 to 26.3 feet!

These very real birds are related to modern-day condors. There is no scientific evidence of their color patterns, and, of course, no proof that they still exist. Teratorns are also put forth as the possible identity of the thunderbird cryptid (see Chapter Four). The prehistoric teratorns are thought to have gone extinct at least 10,000 years ago.

Q: What destructive natural phenomenon could explain Colorado's Slide-Rock Bolter?

A: The answer is in the name: rock slides! If you've ever seen one, they are pretty terrifying, and you'd be forgiven for seeing a monster in the rapidly and fluidly moving rocks and boulders coming down the slope. But trying to blow them up is not recommended (see Chapter Five for one reason you should follow this advice).

Q: What real creature or creatures might account for sightings of the Glastonbury Glawackus?

A: It has been speculated that the Glawackus, an alternately described cat-dog-bear creature sighted in Glastonbury, Connecticut, starting in 1939 (see Chapter Five for more details), may have been a misidentified animal. Some think it was an eastern puma, some other big cat that escaped captivity, and some possibly a bear. But others think it might have been a fisher cat, an animal that fits the bill a little better than any of the others. Fishers (scientific name *Martes pennanti*) are not actually cats but are relatives of weasels, martens, and otters. They typically have dark-brown fur; average thirty-two to forty inches in length, with long, tapered but somewhat bushy tails; and a face that looks like something between a weasel and a tiny bear. Their agile feline-like movements and paw prints might add to the likelihood that a fisher was at least partially to blame for the sightings. Fishers are Indigenous to northern New England, but were largely run out of the area by logging activity in the 1700s and 1800s. An effort to reintroduce them began around the 1950s. It was, in fact, spearheaded by the logging companies, because porcupines were tearing up their newly planted seedlings, and fishers happen to be the only animal that targets porcupines! Fishers are known to prey on smaller farm animals (like chickens), as well as cats and small dogs.

Q: What might account for the Hopkinsville Goblins encounter in Kelly, Kentucky?

A: In 1955 in Kelly, Kentucky, a family had a terrifying encounter with a group of small creatures after one of them believed he saw an alien craft land nearby (see Chapter Five for more details). Skeptic and paranormal researcher Joe

Nickell believes the incident to have been caused by a meteor sighting and an encounter with multiple owls.

Q: Of what supposed sea monster found by a Japanese fishing boat were toys made?

A: In April 1977, the *Zuiyo Maru* was fishing off the coast of Christchurch, New Zealand, when it hauled a huge carcass out of the water. The massive dead beast was thirty-three feet long with a small head, long neck, and four large flippers. Crew members snapped photographs and took samples, but the rotting carcass was ultimately tossed overboard. It drew media attention with some stating that it looked like the long-extinct plesiosaur. This sparked the public imagination, and toys of the Zuiyo Maru Monster were even released. But based on analysis of the samples, it was determined to most likcly be the body of a dead basking shark.

Q: What creature do some believe might account for the Amazonian Mapinguari legends?

A: Although as far as we know there has never been an animal with a large, toothy mouth on its abdomen (see Chapter Six for more on this deadly beast), there is one extinct animal that hits some of the descriptive markers of the Mapinguari: the giant ground sloth (*Mylodontidae*). The ground sloth was a large, hairy creature with long, hooked claws on its hands and feet that was present in the Amazon. Some researchers, however, find this connection unlikely because the stories of the Mapinguari seem to have sprung up more recently than if they were from ancestral memories of extinct sloths.

Q: What real animal might account for a famous sighting of a suspected baby Cadborosaurus?

A: A cryptid called Cadborosaurus (nicknamed Caddy) has been reported up and down the coast of the Pacific Northwest in North America (see the Cadborosaurus entry in Chapter Three, "Deep Water: Sea Serpents, Lake Monsters, and Other Water Dwellers," for more details). In 1968, Captain William Hagelund caught a scaly sixteen-inch-long sea creature with a thin body and flippers that he believed to be a baby sea serpent (although he didn't keep it for analysis). Modern skeptics have suggested that what he really caught was a pipefish, which is a relative of the seahorse that fits a similar description.

Q: What real-life creature do some believe Tahoe Tessie actually was?

A: At least one sighting of Tahoe Tessie, swimming beneath a water-skier, was described as a huge black or gray fish that measured at least ten feet long. Some believe that perhaps someone released a sturgeon into the lake, which are prehistoric fish that still exist today and can grow up to twelve feet in length. They are also bottom-feeders, and thus could remain hidden most of the time. The drop in sightings after the 1980s could be accounted for by an animal that existed but then died.

Q: What real-life toothy fish is the likely identity of the Lake Erie Chomper?

A: In 2001, three swimmers (one a child) went to the beach at Port Dover over two days and left with vicious bite marks (see Chapter Three for more details). The bite marks matched the dental status of the bowfin, a still-extant prehistoric fish from the Triassic era that has a lot of very sharp teeth and will eat just about anything. Or will try, at least. Fortunately for us, it's not big enough to take down a human.

Q: The existence of what seal-like creature was suggested by a famous cryptozoologist to explain some sea monster sightings?

A: Famous founding cryptozoologist Bernard Heuvelmans suggested that many sea monster sightings could give reason to believe in the existence of what he called the "long-necked sea-serpent," which he gave the scientific name *Megalotaria longicollis*. Heuvelmans described the hypothetical beast as being anywhere from seven to thirty meters in length with brown skin; a long, flexible neck; a small seal-like or camel-like head; four large flippers; and a dorsal ridge. Indeed, he believed the creature to possibly be a giant relative of the pinnipeds (which means "flipper-footed" and is the group to which the four-flippered seals, sea lions, and walruses belong). Other cryptozoologists have referred to the creature as the long-necked seal. But there have been no actual sightings and no fossils found to back up the hypothesis.

Q: What visual and psychological phenomenon could account for some cryptid sightings?

A: The human brain is a complex organ that jumps through hoops to interpret the information fed to it via our five senses, including vision. One phenomenon that might account for some sightings is pareidolia. This is our tendency to look at random visual elements and see more specific shapes in them, like seeing animals in the clouds, faces in stained surfaces, or even the face of Jesus on a piece of toast. The same can go for the various organic shapes of foliage, trees, rocks, and other things out in the woods, which could lead to some sightings.

Q: What are possible scientific explanations for the Scottish mountain-dwelling cryptid the Big Gray Man?

A: The Big Gray Man (also known as Am Fear Liath Mor) is a tall, gray, hairy bipedal cryptid associated with the Scottish mountains Ben Macdui and Braeriach (see Chapter Two, "Getting Hairy: Bigfoot, the Yeti, and other Furry Hominids," for more information). The creature often appears as an incredibly tall, gray figure surrounded by mist. One possible visual phenomenon that might account for this is called a Brocken spectre, in which certain conditions involving light and clouds cause the enormously enlarged shadow of a climber to be cast onto low clouds. Many who have reported the cryptid also said that they felt they were being followed and were overtaken by a sudden sense of fear or dread. Psychological phenomenon such as mountain panic (sudden fear that sometimes occurs in wild natural settings such as on a mountain) and the sense-presence effect (the perception of another presence nearby, reported by mountain climbers and other endurance athletes), could account for these feelings. See below for a mountain sound effect that might also come into play in some cryptid sightings.

Q: What are possible natural causes that could explain the Dark Watchers of the Central California coast?

A: The Dark Watchers are tall, dark silhouette-like humanoid figures reported to stand silently looking over the area in the Santa Lucia mountains in Central California (see Chapter Six for more detail). One possible explanation is that they are an illusion caused by light and the mountainous terrain. As with the Big Gray Man, the Brocken spectre might be at work in these tall, shadowy figure sightings (see above). The fact that they usually appear at dusk or dawn lends that idea some credence, although there have been sightings outside those times. Another is that the wind blowing against the rocks in the area can cause infrasound signals, which are known to affect the brain.

Q: What natural occurrences common to deep lakes might account for some lake creature sightings?

A: Differences and changes in water temperature in deep lakes can lead to the sudden appearance of waves, a phenomenon called "thermal stratification," which happens when denser water moves underneath less dense water. People also might be seeing mirages on the surface that they interpret as the presence of a lake creature. And for those large, ten-foot or so creatures some people see swimming under the surface, there are fish that large, most notably sturgeons.

Q: What real cat species is thought by some to perhaps explain the Mngwa?

A: The Mngwa is a large as yet unclassified gray cat that has been reported to attack people in the Lindi and Mchinga areas on the coast of Tanzania (see Chapter Six for more on this ferocious felid). Some, including cryptozoologist Bernard Heuvelmans, have postulated that it may be an undiscovered (by science) subspecies of the species *Profelis aurata*, also known as the African golden cat, which roams in Kenya and Uganda (although it is not known to live in Tanzania). Despite the name, African golden cats can apparently vary in color, and some are even gray, like the cat from the reported Mngwa sightings.

Q: What could account for the presence of a large cat or cats in Exmoor in the UK since the 1970s?

A: In 1976, the United Kingdom passed the Dangerous Wild Animals Act (sometimes referred to as the Exotic Pets Act), which made it illegal to keep potentially dangerous animals as pets without a government-issued license and other controls. It has been postulated that perhaps someone released one or more big cats (such as leopards or pumas) in the Exmoor area in the 1970s before their ownership became illegal or costly, leading to the spate of big cat sightings that have since plagued the area.

Q: What was the Gloucester Sea Serpent likely in reality?

A: Joe Nickell, senior research fellow for the Committee for Skeptical Inquiry, delved into the sighting accounts of the Gloucester Sea Serpent and believes it was actually a school of narwhals, themselves a rare sea creature that looks like something out of a fairy tale! The narwhal is a whale, closely related to the beluga whale. Narwhals measure up to eighteen feet long, travel in groups, and many, especially the males, have a long spear-like horn protruding from their foreheads. Observers quite possibly saw the lead narwhal's head and horn, and perceived all the following narwhals to be humps on the same creature. Their speed and ability to dive quickly fit the bill. They also do something called "logging," where they lie still and float for hours, which may, along with their dappled gray coloration, account for their name (*nár* is Old Norse for "corpse," making narwhal translate to "corpse whale"). And a few of the Gloucester accounts described seeing a school of whales rather than one giant creature. Narwhals typically inhabit the waters of the Arctic, but it is quite possible that they took occasional jaunts to Massachusetts to baffle lookers-on in the early nineteenth century.

Q: What sea creatures were often mistaken for mermaids?

A: Many people at sea have reported mermaid sightings (the half-woman, half-fish creatures of mythology), including Christopher Columbus himself, who believed he saw one in 1492 on his way to "discover" America. But most of these sightings are actually of manatees (or their close relatives, dugongs). In fact, Columbus's mermaid report is now considered the first written account of manatees in North America.

Q: What large water-dwelling creatures are confirmed to live in Lake Ikeda in Japan?

A: Lake Ikeda is known for the cryptid Issie. But it is also home to a scientifically recognized creature—giant unagi (freshwater) eels. These large sea creatures have been known to reach over six feet long! Sightings of these oversized aquatic fauna could account for some monster sightings in the lake.

Q: What real prehistoric creature do some cryptozoologists believe the Bigfoots, Yetis, Yeren, and other hairy ape-men of the world to be?

A: During the Pleistocene epoch (which lasted from 2.6 million to 11,700 years ago), a large ape standing three meters (nearly ten feet) high and aptly called *Gigantopithicus blacki* roamed the area that is now southern China. The creature is believed to have gone extinct around 300,000 years ago. Some fossils that might be related were also found in Thailand and Vietnam, although whether they truly are

G. blacki hasn't been established yet. Bones and teeth of the enormous beast have been found in several areas in China, including some where the Yeren is said to roam. Giganto-pithecus is believed to share a common ancestor with modern orangutans. The extinct behemoth is put forward by some cryptozoologists as what Bigfoot, the Yeti, the Yeren and other similar hairy hominids might actually be, and other cryptozo-oologists believe that Gigantopithecus still exists as a taller and larger separate cryptid from Bigfoot and its brethren, dubbed True Giants.

Q: What disease may have accounted for much of the early vampire lore?

A: The tales of vampirism that came out of the Slavic regions during the 1700s included symptoms, both before and after death, that seemed very odd to people at the time. In stories of vampirism that came out of Serbia in the 1730s, the assumed vampires would attack and bite people like an animal, and once dead, would seem not to decompose very quickly, and their blood didn't coagulate (facts that would become known once a suspected vampire was exhumed from the grave). These pre-death and postmortem symptoms can be caused by the rabies virus, and there was a reported rabies outbreak in the area in the 1720s. Rabies also might account for the fact that vampires were said to be able to turn into wolves and bats, two animals that are known to contract and transmit rabies.

Q: What real creatures might account for Bunyip sightings and legends?

A: Some Bunyip sightings are attributed to seals, as the creature is often described as seal-like (although the descriptions are all over the place). As to the creature's fearsome roar, the call of the bittern marsh bird is one possible culprit.

As to animals that might have led to the Bunyip lore, some have suggested that early encounters with nonnative animals like water buffalos and other cattle brought by British colonizers, who began their encroachment in 1788, might have played a role. And others posit that ancestral stories from early encounters with a real prehistoric creature from Australia's past may have been the inspiration. The Diprotodon, also called the giant wombat, was a fur-covered quadrupedal marsupial that could reach about six feet tall and twelve feet long (about the size of a large rhinoceros). Its closest living relatives are wombats and koala bears. These giant wombats are thought to have gone extinct around 46,000 years ago. Australia's Aboriginal people arrived on the continent over 50,000 years ago (perhaps even as early as 70,000 years ago), so it's quite possible they had encounters with the creature and passed the stories down through the ages. But it is also very possible that it is something from a First Nations' Dreamtime story (Aboriginal creation stories) and not based on a real animal.

Q: What real affliction could account for jackalope sightings?

A: The North American horned-rabbit cryptid the jackalope demonstrably started as a hoax (see Chapter Eight for more info), but supposed sightings of the creatures have a possible real-world basis. Although there are no rabbits with antlers (which are made of bone), there is a virus that can cause rabbits to grow something similar to horns (which are made of keratin rather than bone). A rare virus called papillomatosis can cause Shope papilloma in rabbits, which causes them to develop keratin growths on random parts of their bodies. This might account for some horned rabbit sightings.

Q: What do experts believe the Delhi Monkey Man to have been in reality?

A: A group called the Indian Rationalist Association investigated and found that the wounds attributed to the Monkey Man (see Chapter Two for the full story) were not uniform from person to person, and many were likely self-inflicted. There was otherwise no physical evidence of the creature. They believe the Monkey Man panic was a case of mass sociogenic illness (aka mass hysteria), where the idea and panic were spread by suggestion from person to person.

Q: What diseases could account for some Not Deer sightings?

A: A disease called epizootic hemorrhagic disease (EHD) has broken out in deer populations in some of the areas known for Not Deer sightings. Another possible culprit is chronic wasting disease (CWD). Both ailments can cause deer to become emaciated and exhibit neurological symptoms that affect movement. The former can also cause head and neck swelling, and the latter a blank expression on the deer's face, and excessive drooling. All of these symptoms can make a deer look odd to an observer.

Q: What Pleistocene-era animal thought to have gone extinct was discovered alive and well in Paraguay in the 1970s?

A: The Chacoan peccary (*Parachoerus wagneri*), also known as the Pecarí or Tagua chaqueño, was confirmed by scientists to have existed in the Pleistocene era (around 2.6 million to 11,700 years ago) due to the fossil record. The creature was thought extinct, but rumors of their demise were much exaggerated. In the early 1970s, zoologist Ralph Wetzel found a group of living Chacoan peccaries in Paraguay. They are spiky-haired pig- or boar-like animals that inhabit the Gran Chaco plains of northern Argentina, southeastern Bolivia, and western Paraguay. Chacoan peccaries are omnivores that eat fleshy plants, fruits, seeds, roots, and small mammals, among other things. They are considered a threatened species, with only an estimated five thousand in existence as of 1990.

Q: What real-world living things were once considered cryptids?

A: Many creatures were at some point considered nonexistent or folkloric by scientists but were known to exist by Indigenous peoples in the areas the creatures inhabited. For instance, scientists didn't know that gorillas were real until 1847. And they didn't know about mountain gorillas, which were reported by locals as ape-men living in the mountains, until 1902. An animal becomes recognized in the field of zoology once a living or dead specimen has been found and examined. Here are some other animals (and one plant) that were considered imaginary until they were found, and the year they entered the scientific record:

- Microscopic organisms (i.e., germs), 1676
- Pelican, 1758
- Venus flytrap, 1759
- Kangaroo, 1770
- Platypus, 1799
- Giant panda, 1869
- King of Saxony Bird-of-Paradise, late-nineteenth century
- Okapi, 1901
- Komodo dragon, 1912

- Bonobo (aka pygmy chimpanzee), 1929
- Coelacanth (Cretaceous era fish thought to have gone extinct), 1938
- Megamouth shark, 1976
- Giant gecko, 1984
- Beaked whale, 1991
- Spindle-horn ox, 1992
- Arunachal macaque, 1997
- Diane's bare-hearted glass frog, 2015 (a frog that resembles Kermit!)

Q: In what area in Southeast Asia were multiple previously undocumented animals discovered starting in 1992?

A: Vũ Quang is a rural region in Vietnam that borders Laos at the Annamite mountains. In 1992, scientists there discovered the *Saola Pseudoryx nghetinhensis,* a large bovine animal that was previously undocumented, and was in fact the first new mammal discovered in decades at the time. The saola has brown hair, white facial markings, and two long, straight horns on its head (present on males and females). In 1994, a sort of deer, the Giant Muntjac *Megamuntiacus vuquangensis,* was also discovered in the region. Other new animals have since been discovered, some pending scientific classification.

Q: What apparently bipedal sea creature washed ashore in England in the 1950s?

A: In 1953 and then in 1954, two bizarre specimens of dead sea creature washed ashore at Canvey Island in Essex, England. They were collectively dubbed the Canvey Island Monster. The first was nearly a meter long and the second was over a meter long. They appeared to have large hind limbs, each with five toes, as well as gills and bulging eyes. People thought they had stumbled upon some unknown aquatic bipedal creature. But the two carcasses turned out to be those of decaying anglerfish, aka monkfish (scientific name *Lophius piscatorius*), which are, indeed, pretty bizarre-looking fish that can reach up to two meters in length, but they are fairly common and known to inhabit the area where they washed ashore, and they have fins, not limbs.

Q: What real animal-eating plants exist?

A: The Venus flytrap is likely the best known flesh-devouring plant, which traps flies, spiders, other insects, and arachnids in its clam-like mouths, which are two leaves with hinges that spring shut when something touches hairlike trichomes on the inner surface of each leaf pair more than once. The leaf edges have bristles that look a little like teeth, but they really serve as bars to keep the plant's prey from escaping as it digests each hapless tiny animal over several days. It also gets energy through photosynthesis, and produces white flowers. Venus flytraps are native to North and South Carolina in the United States. Another is a Malaysian plant called the "Nepenthes rajah," referred to as a "pitcher plant" because its bulk resembles a pitcher and actually does hold several liters of fluid, although the fluid is a mix of water and digestive fluids. Unlike the Venus flytrap, the N. rajah doesn't have moving parts. Insects and small animals, up to and including rats, get lured by the scent, fall into the pitcher, and get trapped and digested. They are known to attract tree shrews, too, but fortunately for the shrews, these little mammals use them as toilets and scurry off. Their feces provide nutrients to the plant without requiring it to kill anything. Napenthes rajah and its smaller cousin Napenthes rafflesiana are the only known plants that kill and eat mammals on occasion.

Q: What real creature that sometimes walks on two legs is thought to be responsible for some Yeti sightings?

A: Yeti footprints are often attributed to wolves, but actual Yeti sightings may have another culprit: the Himalayan brown bear (*Ursus arctos isabellinus*)—this large, hairy animal is sometimes known to stand on its hind legs.

Q: What real animal do some believe Champ to be?

A: The Lake Champlain monster Champ has sometimes been described as a very large and long fish. Some believe Champ sightings to actually be sightings of a particularly lengthy garfish, which is a fish with an elongated jaw that sports lots of scary-looking sharp teeth.

Q: What animal was Steller's Sea Ape most likely?

A: In 1741 while on the Second Kamchatka Expedition helmed by Commander Vitus Bering, naturalist Georg Wilhelm Steller saw an animal he had never seen before near Bering Island, a member of the Aleutian Islands off the southwestern coast of Alaska. From the expedition ship, Steller saw a five-foot-long animal with a head like a dog's, large eyes, long downward-pointing whiskers, thick gray fur on its back, reddish-white fur on its underside, and a round body that tapered toward the back into what he described as a tail divided into two flippers. He wrote that the animal swam playfully around the ship for two hours, and noted that it could keep about one third of its body out of the water for a few minutes at a time, and that he couldn't see any forelimbs or front flippers. He had apparently never seen a northern fur seal, which fits his description quite well, especially the female of the species (due to the described coloration and size). Its front flippers rest further back than those of many other seals, so they probably remained out of sight, and the divided tail was likely the seal's two individual rear flippers. Stellar said he shot at the creature twice (to take it as a specimen), but thankfully for the seal, he missed.

Q: What type of chimera really exists?

A: A chimera is a mythical creature made up of multiple animals, usually depicted with a lion's head, a goat's body and a dragon's tail. This creature never existed. But there are chimeras that do exist. They are any animal that has sets of DNA from more than one individual. There are even human chimeras. This can happen after a bone marrow transplant, when fraternal (non-identical) twins in the womb swap cells via connected placentas, or when one fraternal twin is absorbed by another in the womb. A phenomenon called microchimerism can occur after blood transfusion or organ transplants, or when pregnant women and their fetuses swap cells via the placenta. Sometimes this is temporary and sometimes more permanent. Fetal cells have been detected in at least one woman at the age of ninety-four. This can result in some of a woman's cells containing Y chromosomes from their male children.

Q: What real bird of North America became a cryptid recently?

A: The ivory-billed woodpecker, also called the Lord God Bird, is an animal that used to exist, but it was last confirmed alive in 1944. In 2021, the US Fish and Wildlife Service announced plans to declare the bird extinct. And now it fits the description of a cryptid, because there are people who firmly believe that the ivory-billed woodpecker is still flying around the country, and there have even been sightings. Some experts believe that some of the witnesses are actually seeing a similar non-extinct bird called the pileated woodpecker.

Q: What real striped, furry creature native to islands off the Australian continent is now a cryptid?

A: The Thylacine (*Thylacinus cynocephalus*), often called the Tasmanian tiger or Tasmanian wolf, was a canine-like marsupial with light fur punctuated by dark vertical stripes across its back. Related to the Tasmanian devil, the Thylacine did exist, but the last known example of its species died in 1936. However, people still report sightings of the creature on the islands of Tasmania and New Guinea, and sometimes in Australia. So who knows? Maybe one day this creature will be rediscovered like the Chacoan peccary (see more on these plucky porcine pals earlier in this chapter).

Q: What large bat species went extinct in the 1800s?

A: *Desmodus draculae*, aka the giant vampire bat, once inhabited South and Central America, and fossils have even been found as far north as Mexico in southern North America. Its heyday was from the Pleistocene epoch to the Holocene epoch, but the last known giant vampire bats died out as recently as 1820. Like its modern living vampire bat relatives, it fed on the blood of animals (up to and including humans). The "giant" in the name probably makes them sound like monsters, but they were only giant compared to other bats. *Desmodus draculae* had a wingspan of around twenty inches, compared to the average wingspan of a modern vampire bat, around 7 inches. Like many recently extinct creatures, some believe they are still alive somewhere out there.

Q: What small elephants have inspired a debate about whether or not they are their own species?

A: The African pygmy elephant, described as a small elephant no taller than 6.5 feet, with reddish hair and thought to be more aquatic than their forest and bush counterparts, is considered a cryptid by many. Classified by German scientist Theodore Noack in 1906 and given the scientific name *Loxodonta pumilio*, there has been debate over the last century as to whether these small elephants were their own separate species or just a subgroup of the African forest elephant (*Loxodonta cyclotis*). The forest elephants are smaller than the other known species of elephant on the continent of Africa, the bush elephant (*Loxodonta africana*). And multiple researchers over the decades have argued that these smaller pygmy elephants are a third African species of elephant, including famous cryptozoologist Bernard Heuvelmans. A 2003 study by researchers at the French National Museum of Natural History (*Muséum national d'histoire naturelle*) concluded that the so-called pygmy elephants are, in fact, forest elephants, and that some of the diversity seen across the species could be accounted for by separation of populations across different climates.

Q: What bird was likened to a phoenix by news reports when it was brought back from the brink of extinction?

A: The Japanese crested ibis, called the *toki* in Japanese, is native to Sado, a small island off the west coast of mainland Japan. The toki, known to live around rice paddies, are thought to have been greatly reduced in number because they were being hunted for their meat (said to have healing properties) and their attractive feathers. Later, the use of pesticides on rice crops pushed them even closer to extinction. The wild toki all but disappeared, and the last five known wild toki were taken into captivity in 1981 by the government to protect them. As far as anyone knew, only specimens in captivity remained, and they weren't breeding successfully. The last one died in 2003 at the ripe old age of thirty-six! But as luck would have it, seven wild toki were found in the Shaanxi province of China. These birds were bred more successfully. In 1998, during the first-ever visit to Japan of a Chinese head of state, president of China Jiang Zemin offered to give Japan a pair of toki. These birds, named You You and Yang Yang, had an offspring. Additional birds were sent from China, and Japan was able to breed more. They also had local farmers cut back on pesticide use. The toki were released back into the wild on Sado Island in 2008. There are now an estimated 480 toki in the area, and many news reports of the bird's successful comeback likened them to modern-day phoenixes.

Q: What real creatures might account for tales of the Orang Bati?

A: The Orang Bati is a flying monkey-like creature reportedly inhabiting the island of Seram in Indonesia (see Chapter Four for more details). Some experts postulate that misinterpreted sightings of a very real creature, giant fruit bats (also known as flying foxes), might account for some tales of this flying child-stealing monster. Although only known to inhabit the Philippines, the golden-crowned flying fox has a wingspan of up to five and a half feet! Perhaps it has some cousins in Seram.

Q: What wreckage from a covert government operation led to the belief that the US government is hiding alien bodies from the world?

A: Not all cryptids are of this earth. The town of Roswell, New Mexico, is most remembered for the potentially extraterrestrial activity that officials from the city's Roswell Army Air Field (RAAF) investigated in June or July of 1947. A rancher named W. W. "Mac" Brazel found wreckage of what he thought might be a flying saucer on his property around seventy-five miles north of Roswell in Lincoln County. He brought some of the wreckage to Roswell's sheriff, who contacted the RAAF about it. The RAAF released a statement that they had procured a flying disc from a local rancher. Shortly thereafter, they said that it was actually a weather balloon. This, of course, fanned the flames of conspiracy theories. There were some claims that alien bodies were pulled from the wreckage. In 1994, the Air Force released a statement saying that it was actually a top-secret device for spying on the Soviets as part of an operation called Project Mogul, which included microphones and high-altitude balloons. Despite this plausible explanation, these events have fueled speculation that the US government has been hiding the truth of alien visits all along. See Chapter Eight to find out about a televisual event that added to rampant speculation about the alien bodies supposedly recovered from the Roswell crash.

Q: What real creature might have inspired tales of the hoop snake?

A: The hoop snake is a snake that is reported to put its tail in its mouth in order to roll after its prey and then unfurl itself to sting with its tail (see Chapter Six for more info). Some think that the hoop snake was inspired by a real snake called the mud snake (scientific name *Farancia abacura*). Found in the Coastal Plains of the United States (from eastern Texas to Florida and up to Virginia) and up the Mississippi to southern Illinois, these nonvenomous aquatic snakes have a spinelike scale at the end of their tails and are known to press this spiny tip against those who capture them, possibly making people think they have a stinger (which they don't). They are also said by some to be able to curl up and roll like a hoop snake, but there is no evidence that this is true. They slither and swim like the typical aquatic snake.

Q: **What giant extinct shark do some believe still exists?**

A: The Megalodon (scientific name *Otodus megalodon*) was a giant shark that lived from around 20 million to 3.6 million years ago, when it went extinct. The Megalodon is thought to have measured up to sixty feet in length (an estimate based on its tooth fossils, which measure up to about seven inches in length). For comparison, the longest recorded great white shark measured around twenty feet long. Some people hold out hope that the Meg still exists in the wild, just waiting to be found—or to find us.

Chapter 8

FAKING IT

FAMOUS HOAXES

Q: What made-up lumberjack-eating monster was once thought to roam Wisconsin?

A: Lumberjack and surveyor Eugene Shepard told tales of a beast who would eat his fellow lumberjacks in the Northwoods area of Rhinelander, Wisconsin, in the late 1800s. Named the Hodag of Wisconsin, the creature was described as large and stocky, with a hideous face, sharp fangs and claws, enormous horns, and a spiky tail. The beast was said to have sprung from the ashes of cremated oxen that died hauling loads for the lumber companies, and that, oddly enough, it could be felled by lemons and other citrus fruit. Shepard even had an apparent captive Hodag that he exhibited at fairs in a curtained stall that he wouldn't let people stand near too long. He later revealed that the captive Hodag was carved out of wood and that he had made up the whole story, including all reported sightings. But the cryptid continues on as a part of the area's folklore, including as a statue in front of the Rhinelander Visitor Center.

Q: What part of a Bunyip was supposedly brought back by an expedition of European colonizers in 1846?

A: In 1846, an expedition went out in search of a Bunyip and came back with what they said was the skull of the creature. But experts believe it to have been the modified skull of a cow or horse. The skull was subsequently "lost," adding to further doubts of its authenticity.

Q: What late-1800s account of a man-eating tree turned out to be entirely fictitious?

A: Starting around the 1870s or 1880s, some believed in the existence of the Devil Tree of Madagascar, also called

Crinoida Dajeeana, due to a highly detailed account supposedly given by a German explorer named Karl Liche. He and another explorer were said to have been shown a tree called the "tepe" by the Mkodos tribe of Madagascar and witnessed the sacrifice of a woman handed over to the tree. The tepe was described as having a thick, almost pineapple-like trunk; very long leaves with sharp points at the ends; a bowl-like appendage that contained an intoxicating liquid; and long, tentacle-like tendrils that would ensnare and kill its victims. British cryptozoologist Dr. Karl Shuker referenced the account, and several explorers looked for the killer plant in Madagascar. But in 1888, a new magazine, *Current Literature*, reprinted the original story by Edmund Spencer, which he had originally written for *New York World* newspaper in 1874. The reprinting revealed that the entire story was fictitious, including the plant, the explorer names, and the Madagascar tribe.

Q: What supposedly giant man was "found" in upstate New York in 1869?

A: In 1867, cigar maker and skeptic George Hull got into a debate about religion with a preacher who believed in a literal interpretation of the Bible, including the belief that giant people once inhabited the earth. Hull hatched a scheme to have a ten-foot-tall statue carved out of a chunk of gypsum. He and the sculptors attempted to make it look real, faking pores with pinpricks and distressing it with sulfuric acid to age it. Hull then had it buried on William Newell's farm (a relative of his) in Cardiff, New York. Apparently a patient man, Hull left it there for an entire year, then had Newell hire someone to dig a well and "discover" the three-thousand-pound giant. The discovery caused a stir, drew crowds, and worked up debate about whether it was a petrified man or an ancient statue. Newell charged admission to see it and then sold a large stake in the endeavor to a group of businessmen for $30,000. Having paid $3,000 to create the thing, Hull did pretty well with his cut of the admission charges and the sale. After passing through a few hands, the giant was eventually sold to the Farmers' Museum in Cooperstown, New York, where it still resides.

Q: What bit of treachery did P. T. Barnum contribute to the story of the Cardiff Giant?

A: Even as experts were declaring the Cardiff Giant a fake, famous showman P. T. Barnum tried to purchase the sculpture from the new owners, who refused to sell. Rather than take no for an answer, Barnum hired someone to sculpt an exact copy of the statue and placed it in a museum in Manhattan as the Cardiff Giant, and reportedly made even more money with the fake of the fake than the original fake made in Cardiff. By 1870, several more replicas were made and displayed in other places. Eventually the public lost interest in any of the Cardiff Giants.

Q: What hoax was perpetrated by an Orlando newspaper?

A: In 1984, the *Orlando Sentinel* ran a story about the so-called Tasmanian mock walrus, a supposed creature that made a good pet and ate cockroaches as a bonus. The story was replete with a photo of the creature, and it prompted people to make calls looking for this friendly roach-exterminating animal. But the picture was actually of a naked mole rat, and the Tasmanian mock walrus was just that—mock. The fact that the article was published on April 1 was one major clue to the tallness of the tale. The story even reached the supposed natural habitat of the mock walrus: a Tasmanian newspaper printed a story about the joke.

Q: What fake cephalopod was purported to have washed up on a beach in Santa Monica in 2014?

A: In January 2014, an article with a picture of a giant 160-foot-long squid appeared on the site Lightly Braised Turnip. For comparison, the largest giant squid known to science was just under forty-three feet long. Some people fell for the article, but Lightly Braised Turnip (now defunct) was a satire site kind of like *The Onion*, but less obvious. And the photo was a skillful Photoshop job that combined the photo of a real giant squid that washed up on a beach in Spain and a picture of a whale that washed up on a beach in Chile. The Spanish squid was placed on the Chilean beach, and voila! The 160-foot hoax was born.

Q: What famous "proof" of Nessie's existence turned out to be a hoax?

A: Likely the most famous photograph of the Loch Ness Monster was published by the *Daily Mail* in 1934, purportedly taken by Lieutenant Colonel Robert Kenneth Wilson (see Chapter Three for more backstory). In 1975, a confession by Ian Wetherell was printed in the *Sunday Telegraph* in which he admitted it was a hoax perpetrated by him and his father, Marmaduke Wetherell (a big-game hunter who had perpetrated a Loch Ness Monster footprint hoax in December 1933 using a dried hippopotamus foot), and Marmaduke's stepson, Christian Spurling. Spurling confirmed the hoax story in the 1990s: Ian and Christian had made the model by attaching a fake head and neck to a toy submarine. The group of hoaxers placed it in the water at Loch Ness, and Ian took photos with a

Leica camera. The photo was given by a collaborator, Maurice Chambers, to Wilson, who gave it to the *Daily Mail* for publication. And this fake photo propelled Nessie to worldwide fame.

Q: What turned out to be the cause of the famous Bluff Creek Valley footprints attributed to Bigfoot?

A: In 1958, construction workers found large footprints in the Bluff Creek Valley area in California, and one made plaster casts of the prints, which prompted the story that gave this famous North American hairy hominid the moniker Bigfoot (read more about this in Chapter Two, "Getting Hairy: Bigfoot, the Yeti, and Other Furry Hominids"). Bigfoot became a sensation in the United States and all over the world. But in 2002, the culprit behind the footprints was revealed. Upon the death of Ray Wallace in 2002, his children revealed that their father had created the footprints himself as a prank. And the rest was history.

Q: What cryptid dress-up hoax was perpetrated by a newspaper editor and an actor in the 1960s?

A: In Selbyville, Delaware, in the 1960s, editor of the *Delmarva News* Ralph Grapperhaus had his actor friend Fred Stevens concoct a Bigfoot-like costume (reportedly consisting of a club, a mask, and a raccoon hat that belonged to his Aunt Dorothy), hide in the tree line on Route 54, and jump out to scare passersby. The performance was apparently convincing, because the legend of the Selbyville Swamp Monster was born. Although it probably didn't hurt that the *Delmarva News* printed stories about the beast. The creature was believed to roam the Great Cypress Swamp. Despite the fact that Stevens finally admitted to his and Grapperhaus's ruse in 1987, people still continued to report sightings of the creature.

Q: What video of the Michigan Dogman turned out to be skillful fakery?

A: In 2006, Michigan DJ Steve Cook claimed to have received a reel of 8 mm film that was reportedly part of a lot bought at an estate sale by an elderly woman. A tag on the film said "Gable Case," which is why the video is now known as the "Gable Film." He posted the footage on the web. The three-and-a-half-minute film consists of random home-movie footage, including several shots of kids riding snowmobiles, a man chopping wood, and a (perfectly ordinary) dog sniffing around in the snow, but ends with a creature spotted on the side of the road. The cameraman gets out of the car and a hairy creature runs at the camera on all fours. The camera-man seems to run, the mouth of an animal with sharp teeth fills the frame, and the camera falls to the ground and lies still in the brush. From the vehicles, clothing, and film quality, it appeared to have been shot in the 1970s. But it turned out to be a skillful fake created in 2007 by a machinist named Mike Agrusa with help from his family using a vintage 8 mm camera and 1970s vehicles from his own collection. Mike Agrusa himself donned a ghillie suit (a type of camouflage suit worn by soldiers and hunters that is covered in loose strips of material meant to resemble foliage) and ran at the camera as the monster. The next year, he created a second video that purported to show the police investigation of the crime scene that shows that the cameraman was torn in half. Agrusa was inspired in part by a song he remembered from his youth, which you can read about in Chapter Ten.

Q: What did the Georgia Bigfoot turn out to actually be?

A: In July 2008, two Georgia men, Matthew Whitton and Rick Dyer, claimed that they had found the body of a Bigfoot while on a hike in North Georgia in June, and that they had seen live ones on their way out with the body. They reportedly froze the body to preserve it, and sold it for $50,000 to Searching for Bigfoot, Inc., run by Bigfoot-hunter Tom Biscardi. Whitton, Dyer, and Biscardi held a press conference displaying the frozen creature and promising proof that it was real, including DNA evidence. But once thawed, the "body" turned out to be a store-bought costume stuffed with dead animal remains and frozen. The two men claimed it was all a joke gone awry. The two were also apparently trying to start a Bigfoot tracking business. Whitton lost his job as a police officer over the hoax.

Q: What live cryptid was part of the Ringling Bros. and Barnum & Bailey Circus in the 1980s?

A: In 1984, Ringling Bros. and Barnum & Bailey Circus, the self-dubbed "Greatest Show on Earth," introduced what had only before been a mythical creature: the unicorn! Four "unicorns" were put on display around the country as part of their act. These were actual live creatures, each with a single horn growing from the middle of its head like the unicorns of lore. But unlike the mythical creature's most common depiction, instead of resembling horses, they resembled goats. The circus talked about them like they were real mythical unicorns, but it was later revealed that the uni-horns didn't come naturally to the animals. When the goats were kids (baby goats), their natural dual horn buds were surgically manipulated toward the center, so instead of two horns on either side of their heads, they grew one horn in the middle. In the sense of the word unicorn (in Latin, *uni-* means "one" and *corn* means "horn"), they were real unicorns. See Chapter

Nine to find out who created the unicorns, and why they were goats instead of horses.

Q: What attempted Bigfoot hoax ended in the death of its perpetrator?

A: In August 2012, a man in Montana, Randy Lee Tenley, donned a military camouflage ghillie suit (which has strands hanging off of it that are supposed to resemble foliage), and stepped onto Highway 93, hoping to cause people to think they were seeing Bigfoot. Tragically, he wasn't easy to see at all, and he was struck by two separate drivers and killed. Friends who were with him revealed that he was trying to perpetrate a Sasquatch hoax.

Q: What "missing link" find in England turned out to be a hoax?

A: In 1912, amateur archeologist Charles Dawson claimed to have found remains of a skull near Piltdown Village in East Sussex, England. The skull was reportedly found in gravel beds from the Pleistocene epoch, which lasted from 2.6 million to 11,700 years ago. Dawson contacted the keeper of geology at the British Museum of Natural History, Arthur Smith Woodward, who reconstructed the skull fragments and surmised that the remains were from a missing link between ape and man who lived around 500,000 years ago. They announced the find at a Geological Society meeting that same year. No one questioned it until 1949, when geologist Dr. Kenneth Oakley, also at the Natural History Museum, used new fluorine-dating tests on the fragments and discovered that they were only 50,000 years old, a time when modern *Homo sapiens* were already in existence. Two experts from Oxford University, anatomist Wilfred Le Gros Clark and anthropologist Dr. Joseph Weiner, determined that the fragments weren't from a single species but from two: one man and one ape, possibly orangutan. The teeth had been filed down and the remains stained. It was all a hoax, only uncovered due to advances in scientific dating technology.

Q: **What famous hoax was believed and written about by Sir Arthur Conan Doyle?**

A: In 1917, during World War I, the families of Frances Griffiths, age nine, and Elsie Wright, age sixteen, moved to Cottingley Beck woods, an idyllic countryside setting in England, while Frances's father was fighting in the war. The girls frequently got in trouble for staying out too late and arriving home covered in dirt. One day, young Frances claimed they stayed out so late because they were distracted by the fairies. Elsie confirmed her story and offered to provide evidence with her amateur photographer father Arthur's camera. The girls took the camera into the woods, Arthur developed the photographs, and they showed the girls frolicking with winged fairies. Arthur believed it was fakery, but Elsie's mother Polly took the photos to a Theosophical Society lecture on fairies and presented them. Society member Edward Gardner had the photos validated by an expert who declared that they hadn't been doctored (but not that the fairies were real). The fairy photos came to the attention of Sir Arthur Conan Doyle, creator of Sherlock Holmes and devoted spiritualist. Doyle and Gardner sent the photos to Kodak, who also found that they weren't doctored, but refused to say they were authentic. With Doyle's help, Gardner went to visit the families in Cottingley and brought along two new cameras to get new photographic evidence. The girls convinced him that the fairies would only appear for children, so they went off into the woods by themselves and took more photos with the fairies. Doyle and Gardner were convinced they were real, and the fairy stories resulted in much debate, many believing them hoaxes but some maintaining belief. In 1983, Elsie and Frances finally admitted that the photos were faked using paper cutouts, although Frances still claimed that one of the photos was real.

Q: What cryptid was likely created by brothers in Wyoming?

A: The story of the jackalope is that in 1939, brothers Douglas and Ralph Herrick of Douglas, Wyoming, bagged a jackrabbit during a hunting trip. Ralph apparently threw the dead rabbit onto the floor and it butted up against a pair of deer antlers. Douglas, who happened to be a taxidermist, mounted the jackrabbit and added the antlers. They began selling these created creatures and they caught on, so much so that Douglas, Wyoming, started referring to itself as the "Jackalope Capital of the World" in tourist brochures in the 1940s. And in 2005, the state legislature made the Jackalope Wyoming's "Official Mythical Creature."

Q: What horned-bunny hybrid predated the jackalope by over a hundred years?

A: The wolpertinger is a cryptid said to call the Bavarian Alps home. It is usually described with the body and head of a hare, the antlers of a deer, and the wings of a bird. As legend would have it, the first wolpertinger was the offspring of a female hare and a male roe deer (roebuck). But the legend really sprang from stuffed creatures made by Bavarian taxidermists in the early 1800s, beginning with a hare with deer antlers and culminating in all sorts of animal-part pairings, including rabbits, deer, pheasants, squirrels, foxes, and even ducks. Like the jackalope, these creations were sold to tourists.

Q: What taxidermied creations were sold as mermaids in the sixteenth century?

A: Jenny Hanivers (aka devilfish) are taxidermied composite creatures that were usually made from the dried bodies of guitarfishes (aka sea bishops, a relative of the ray). Multiple bodies were combined and rearranged to look like undiscovered fanciful creatures and sold to gullible buyers as early as the 1500s. Read on to learn about another type of fake mermaid.

Q: What Japanese taxidermied creations were sold as mermaids?

A: Ningyo were composite creatures made by Japanese taxidermists out of a combination of animal and inanimate materials and passed along as real mummified bodies of mermaids and mermen. Many are still on display in museums throughout the world, including the British Museum, although they are all acknowledged as hoaxes these days.

Q: What supposed sea-dwelling cryptid bodies did P. T. Barnum display in New York?

A: In 1842, famous entertainment mogul P. T. Barnum included a display in Barnum's American Museum in New York that promised to be three bare-chested mermaids. But rather than the titillating sight that was likely expected, museum guests saw three so-called Fiji (or Feejee) mermaids. These were man-made objects created to resemble a fish below the waist and a monkey above.

Q: What supposed cryptid carcass was rumored to belong to a famous actor?

A: The Minnesota Iceman, aka the Siberskoye Creature, was the supposed carcass of a nearly 6-foot-tall Bigfoot-type hairy hominid, frozen in a block of ice and put on display in a glass-topped refrigerator for twenty-five cents per view by Frank D. Hansen as part of a traveling exhibition in the late 1960s. He claimed the specimen had been found off the coast of Siberia and shipped to the US. The carcass drew the attention of zoology student Terry Cullen, cryptozoologists Ivan T. Sanderson, Bernard Heuvelmans (who dubbed it an apparent new species *Homo pongoides*), Mark A. Hall, and Loren Coleman, and even researchers at the Smithsonian Institution. But when the Smithsonian expressed interest in examining the frozen body, no close examination was allowed. The Smithsonian tried to get the FBI involved, but they deemed that no violation of federal law had occurred. They decided to have US customs look into it. Around this time, Hansen said that the "real" body had been replaced with a model replica that was now on display. The Smithsonian called around to prop-making businesses in Hollywood and found one that admitted to creating the iceman model in 1967.

At one point during the debacle, Hansen claimed that he was just displaying the creature for the real owner, a millionaire whose identity he would not disclose. One of the rumored owners was actor James "Jimmy" Stewart of *It's a Wonderful Life* fame. This likely erroneous rumor is not the only connection Jimmy Stewart has to cryptids. Read about another in Chapter Ten, "Pop Goes the Sasquatch: Cryptids in Pop Culture and Media."

Q: What real creature's skeletal remains comprised the supposed aquatic Missouri Leviathan?

A: In 1840, German American fossil collector and showman Albert Koch (self-dubbed Dr. Koch) bought large skeletal remains from a Missouri farmer who had found them on his land. Koch assembled these bones into a thirty-two-foot-long skeleton with upward-pointing horns and presented it as *Missourium* (also called the Missouri Leviathan), an armored aquatic predator that lived in the area alongside man. It really was the skeleton of a prehistoric creature, sort of. *Missourium* was actually made up of the creatively and incorrectly assembled bones of multiple mastodons, large hairy elephant-like land-dwelling creatures that walked the earth alongside humans before dying off during the Ice Age. The remains were bought in 1843 by the British Museum and reassembled correctly into a normal-sized mastodon.

Q: What fraudulent sea serpent skeleton was purchased by King Friedrich Wilhelm IV of Prussia?

A: In 1845, "Dr." Albert Koch (see previous entry on the Missouri Leviathan for more detail) collected the bones of a sea creature near the Tombigbee River in Alabama and constructed them into a massive 114-foot-long sea creature, which he gave the scientific name *Hydrarchos sillimani*. The huge skeleton, which looked like a long, serpentine spine with a large head, was put on display in New York City and then taken on a tour of the country. He ultimately sold the skeleton to Friedrich Wilhelm IV, King of Prussia, who put it on display in the Royal Anatomical Museum in Berlin. But rather than an accurate skeleton of a 114-foot-long sea beast, it was actually a hoax made of the bones of six or so specimens of *Basilosaurus cetoides* (a prehistoric whale erroneously given the *-saurus* suffix, from the Greek word *saûros* meaning "lizard," because it was initially thought to have been a reptile, not a marine mammal), along with some ammonite shells thrown in for good measure.

Koch made a second, ninety-six-foot-long supposed *Hydrarchos* and toured it around, as well. He eventually sold it to J. H. Wood, who put it on display in his Colonel Wood's Museum in Chicago and labeled it *Zeuglodon*, another name for the Basilosaurus whales.

Sadly, both skeletons were destroyed, the former during WWII (although some pieces remain), and the latter during the great fire that swept Chicago in 1871.

Q: What 1995 TV special purported to show aliens from the Roswell crash?

A: In 1995, the Fox network aired a documentary special entitled *Alien Autopsy: Fact or Fiction?* Hosted by Jonathan Frakes of *Star Trek: The Next Generation* fame, it included snippets of a seventeen-minute film purportedly purchased by a British video producer named Ray Santilli and provided to Fox. The film was supposedly US Army footage of the autopsy of an alien body from the famous 1947 UFO crash in Roswell, New Mexico, and it did, indeed, show a graphic autopsy of what looked like the iconic little green man images we have seen for decades. But in 2017, a filmmaker named Spyros Melaris said that Santilli had hired him to create the footage, and that the alien was created by John Humphreys, an FX artist who once worked on the longtime British sci-fi TV series *Doctor Who*.

Q: Which professional race-car driver claimed to have seen a dinosaur-like creature in New Guinea?

A: Adventurer Charles Miller told a story of his time with the Kirrirri tribe in New Guinea (in the 1930s or possibly 1940s), where he heard tales from the tribe of a twelve-meter-long dinosaur-like reptile called the Row (apparently named for the sound it made). He said he disbelieved them until he himself saw a yellowish-brown creature with a turtle-like head, an extremely long neck, short limbs, and armor-like scales. He even claimed to have captured film footage of the beast, and said the locals had large horns from its tail. However, neither the footage nor the horns materialized, and it is thought Miller made the whole thing up. Charles Miller went on to become a professional race-car driver.

Q: An apparent video of what dead, beached cryptid was debunked by the Georgia Department of Natural Resources in 2018?

A: In 2018, a video of the supposed body of an Altamaha-ha sea monster washed up on the beach was submitted to a local news organization, First Coast News, by a Jeff Warren. The video showed a dead creature with a long neck and tail, bulbous middle with two flippers, and some exposed entrails, which appeared to look like the Altamaha-ha sea-monster (see Chapter Three for more details). The Georgia Department of Natural resources examined the video and said it appeared to include footprints that someone tried to wipe away, and that the body looked to be made of papier-mâché and painted, and no actual body was provided as evidence. Also, Jeff Warren ceased contact with the news organization, and when they tried to locate him, they couldn't. There has been speculation that the hoax may have been perpetrated by Taylor Brown, the author of the novel *The River of Kings*, about the Altamaha River area, although he denied his involvement.

Q: What evidence of the Lizard Man of Scape Ore Swamp turned out to be a hoax?

A: The Lizard Man of Scape Ore Swamp in Lee County, South Carolina, terrorized the area from June to July in 1988 (see Chapter Five, "A Bit of Americana: Regional Cryptids of the US"). In August of that year, airman Kenneth Orr of Shaw Air Force Base claimed that he had shot and wounded the Lizard Man on Route 15 and handed in blood and scales as evidence. But it turned out he just didn't want the story of the monster to die off. He admitted it was a hoax during his arraignment for filing a false report and carrying a gun unlawfully.

Q: What cryptid was created on 4chan?

A: In the early 2000s, a cryptid called "the Rake" was reportedly sighted in the Northeast, mostly in Upstate New York. The Rake was described as a tall, pale, hairless, creature that sometimes walked upright, but that usually crouched or moved on all fours. Its face had three eyes and no discernable nose or mouth, until its jaw opened wide to reveal a large number of dull teeth just before it pounced. People cited references to the Rake in a 1691 mariner's journal and an 1880 Spanish journal, among other sources dating all the way back to the twelfth century. But the sources were all fake, as was the creature. The documents and the descriptions of the Rake were all concocted on 4chan in 2005 when one user on a board suggested creating a monster, and others contributed. The story then jumped from 4chan to other platforms like LiveJournal and reddit and took off from there, leading some to believe in the fictitious Rake.

Chapter 9

MONSTER HUNTERS

FAMOUS (AND INFAMOUS) CRYPTOZOOLOGISTS

Q: Who is often called the "father of cryptozoology?"

A: There are actually two zoologists who are often called cryptozoology's fathers or godfathers. Bernard Heuvelmans was born in 1916 and studied zoology at the Free University of Brussels, where he wrote his dissertation on aardvark teeth. One of his mentors was Sergei Isaakovich Freshkop, who believed in bipedalism (the idea that all mammals started out walking upright). Heuvelmans became interested in cryptids before they were called cryptids and wrote the book *Sur la Piste des Bêtes Ignorées* (*On the Track of Unknown Animals*) in 1958.

Heuvelmans was reportedly inspired to pursue the study of cryptids after reading an article written by the other reputed founder of the field, Ivan T. Sanderson. Born in 1911 in Edinburgh, Scotland, Sanderson traveled the world and led expeditions starting in his teen years, studied zoology at Cambridge, and even had his own cryptid sighting in the 1930s (see Chapter Four for more details).

Heuvelmans and Sanderson are considered founding fathers of cryptozoology.

Q: From the name of what researcher of unexplained phenomena did we get the word "fortean?"

A: Charles Hoy Fort was born in 1874 in Albany, New York. As a teen he took a small trust fund his grandfather left him and used it to travel the world for a couple of years. Fort became a writer and researcher of the paranormal. While living in London, he published the *Fortean Times*, a magazine that specializes in tales of the weird and wonderful (including cryptids) and that still exists today online. Fort's magazine inspired the creation of the Fortean Society. The word "fortean" is now an adjective that means having to do with paranormal phenomena. "Forteana" is a related noun meaning paranormal phenomena.

Q: What founding father believed mammoths might still exist in North America?

A: Among the many pursuits of founding father of the United States Thomas Jefferson, one was paleontology. He had new fossils that were discovered in the country brought to him for examination, and some of these were mammoth or mastodon bones. He believed that these creatures were likely to still exist out in the wilderness on parts of the continent that the colonists had not yet explored or taken over.

Q: What future cryptozoologist got his start with the Flatwoods Monster incident?

A: Gray Barker was born on May 2, 1925, in Braxton County in West Virginia, near where the Flatwoods Monster sightings occurred. He got his start investigating and writing about the incident. Barker afterward made a career of researching UFOs, "Men in Black," and cryptids, among other unexplained phenomena. He wrote several books, including his first work, *They Knew Too Much About Flying Saucers*, published in 1956. His second, *The Silver Bridge*, published in 1970, was about the sightings of the Mothman and the collapse of the Silver Bridge in Point Pleasant, West Virginia, in 1967. He passed away on December 6, 1984.

Q: Who drew the first publicized Chupacabra sketch in 1995?

A: In 1995, UFO researcher Jorge Martin drew a sketch of the Puerto Rican cryptid the Chupacabra based on a description from the first Chupacabra eyewitness, Madelyne Tolentino. She described the creature as bipedal, with large eyes and spikes down its back. The sketch looked more like a bipedal alien than the doglike creature that is now more commonly associated with the Chupacabra.

Q: What Austrian doctor wrote an official report of a mass vampire slaying in Serbia in the 1730s?

A: In 1732, Dr. Johannes Flückinger, a surgeon major in the Austrian Army, was dispatched to Medveđa, Serbia, an area that had been transferred from the Ottoman Empire to the Habsburg Empire via treaty in 1718. His mission: to investigate a vampire plague. After a thorough investigation including collection of stories from witnesses, examination of exhumed bodies of suspected vampires, and overseeing the staking, decapitating, and burning of those bodies showing the supposed symptoms of vampirism and disposing of the ashes in a nearby river, he filed a detailed report of the affair that drew the attention of many people across Europe, including Louis XV and that can still be read today.

Q: What spiritualist claimed to have successfully summoned Nessie?

A: In 1977, Salford magician and monster hunter Anthony "Doc" Shiels claimed to have successfully summoned the Loch Ness Monster out of the water near Urquhart Castle using his psychic powers. He even provided photographic evidence, published by the *Daily Mail*, of the creature's head and neck poking out of the water. But like the Nessie pictures that came before, it wasn't entirely convincing.

Q: What paleontologist and inspiration for Indiana Jones brought the Mongolian death worm to the attention of westerners?

A: Paleontologist Professor Roy Chapman Andrews took the helm of the American Museum of Natural History's Central Asiatic Expedition in 1922. They were looking for ancient human fossils, but instead found dinosaur nesting sites, dinosaur eggs, and other scientifically significant finds. But the expedition was also looking for something else. The premier of Mongolia asked Andrews to bring back a Mongolian death worm, and even gave him some protective tools (sunglasses, forceps, and a collection jar). Andrews's crew didn't find the fearsome death worm and indeed believed it likely to be imaginary. He wrote about the Mongolian death worm, among lots of other things, in his book *On the Trail of Ancient Man* published in 1926.

Q: Who was the first Western cryptozoologist known to have launched expeditions looking for the Mongolian death worm?

A: Earlier expeditions of groups went into the Gobi desert looking for human and dinosaur fossils and came back with word-of-mouth anecdotes about the lethal Mongolian death worm. But starting in 1990, Czech cryptozoologist Ivan Mackerle led expeditions into the area specifically to search for the creature.

Q: What cryptozoologist was murdered while looking for the Barmanu?

A: Jordi Magraner was born in 1958 to Spanish parents in Morocco. The family settled in Valence, France, when he was a small child. Magraner became a zoologist. He was influenced by the book *Neanderthal Man Is Still Alive* (*L'homme de Néanderthal est toujours vivant*) by famous cryptozoologist Bernard Heuvelmans and B. F. Porchnev, and corresponded with Heuvelmans about his ideas. In 1987, the young zoologist moved from Fontbarlettes, France, to Chitral, Pakistan, in the Hindu Kush, where he lived among the Kalash people (a religious and ethnic minority in Pakistan). He wandered the area in both Pakistan and nearby Afghanistan gathering accounts from locals of sightings of the Barmanu (the Yeti-like ape-man of the area). In 1994, he and two others traveling in the Shishi Kuh valley in the Chitral mountains apparently heard what they thought sounded like a nonhuman primate but couldn't see it. After 9/11, he trekked to Nuristan, where he was held hostage by an armed group. He was reportedly released after pretending to convert to Islam and returned to his home in Chitral, where he is said to have converted to the Kalash religion. In 2002, apparently just a few weeks before he was to return to France, he was reportedly convinced by one of his servants to visit a village near Afghanistan, where he and his other young servant, a twelve-year-old Kalash boy, were murdered. Their murderer or murderers were never discovered. Magraner was buried in a Kalash graveyard as one of their own.

Q: What religious figure created live "unicorns?"

A: Some people don't just look for mythical creatures—they make them! In 1962, Oberon Zell-Ravenheart cofounded the Church of All Worlds, which was inspired by the Robert A. Heinlein science fiction novel *Stranger in a Strange Land*. Zell-Ravenheart is currently headmaster of the online Grey School of Wizardry, which offers classes on magic, mythology, ancient languages, and other topics. From 1978 to 1985, Oberon Zell and his wife, Morning Glory, created and raised nine "unicorns." Four ended up working for the Ringling Bros. and Barnum & Bailey Circus in 1984 (see Chapter Eight for more info). Zell-Ravenheart developed and patented a process for moving and merging young goats' horn buds toward the center of their heads, from which they would hence grow naturally into one horn. His inspiration was a set of medieval wool-and-silk-woven tapestries now called "The Unicorn Tapestries." The one that particularly influenced him is called "The Unicorn in Captivity," which depicts a unicorn lying in a pen under a tree. The unicorn has a very long horn and a beard. The beard was one reason Zell-Ravenheart chose goats instead of horses, because some goats actually have beards. Another consideration was probably horses' lack of horns.

Q: **What organization keeps a database of Bigfoot and Sasquatch sightings?**

A: The Bigfoot Field Researchers Organization, created in 1995, is a group whose aim is to study the Bigfoot phenomenon and potentially prove its existence. The organization tracks and judges the credibility of alleged Bigfoot and Sasquatch sightings all over the world and keeps the information in a database. Potential sightings can be reported through their website.

Q: **What oil-and-beef magnate and avid cryptozoologist had a relative kidnapped by the gangster Machine Gun Kelly?**

A: As a young man, Thomas Baker Slick Jr. aka Tom Slick, traveled to Scotland in 1937 to look for the Loch Ness Monster. He made his money in the oil and beef businesses, but he never lost his desire to find undiscovered creatures throughout the world. In 1957, he took a trip to Nepal, where he showed photographs of various animals that could be mistaken for Yetis to fifteen people who had reported Yeti sightings. Slick used the information to create a graphical representation of the creature. He also found and took a cast of an apparent Yeti footprint left in mud on the same trip. Slick went on to investigate other cryptids personally and to sponsor the expeditions of fellow cryptid hunters. Despite his unusual pursuits, he was notorious for wishing to avoid publicity, which was perhaps the side effect of too much publicity in his youth. When Slick was a teen in Oklahoma, gangster George Kelly Barnes (aka Machine Gun Kelly) kidnapped his oil-tycoon stepfather, Charles Urschel. Thankfully Urschel was released unharmed after a hefty ransom was paid. The kidnapping propelled Kelly to infamy and ultimately led to his arrest. Tom Slick died in a plane explosion in his forties.

Q: **What Swiss geologist is best known for a faked cryptid photograph?**

A: Born in Switzerland, Louis François Fernand Hector De Loys became a geologist and an oil-prospecting pioneer, traveling the world to survey areas for possible oil fields (including Iraq in 1928, not long after oil was first struck in the country). Despite a fairly successful career (until his untimely death from syphilis in 1935), his profession is not what he is most known for. De Loys was one of several survivors of the failed 1917 Colon Development expedition to the Serranía de Perijá mountains at the border of Venezuela and Colombia in South America. Most of the group disappeared, but in 1920, De Loys and a few others made their way out, and brought with them the photograph that made De Loys famous (or infamous), especially in cryptozoological circles.

The De Loys Ape photo was of a hairy apelike creature sitting upright on a box (with a stick from the ground to its chin seemingly holding it up). De Loys described the creature as one of a pair of erect bipedal apes with no tail and standing around five feet tall that his group encountered in the jungle. He claimed that they shot at the creatures because they were throwing feces at them and that the picture was of the one they killed. He also said that the physical remnants of the specimen had decayed or been lost.

Years after the expedition, the photo came to the attention of an anthropologist friend of De Loys named George-Alexis Montandon, who believed it to be an undiscovered species and publicized the supposed find in 1929 (read on to find out more about Montandon's ulterior motives for publicizing the De Loys photo).

The De Loys missing link photo, however, didn't depict a new species. Even at the time, scientists, including British naturalist Sir Arthur Keith, believed the photographic specimen to be *Ateles belzebuth*, a species of white-bellied spider monkey native to South America. The original photo apparently includes the stumps of human-cultivated banana trees not likely to be found deep in the jungle where De Loys claimed to have taken the photo.

And in 1999, *Interciencia*, a Venezuelan scientific journal, published a letter sent to another magazine in 1962 by Dr. Enrique Tejera who said he worked in De Loys's camp and that the picture was of a monkey that had been given to De Loys alive and well, but with an injured tail, which they cut off. Tejera said that the monkey and De Loys traveled together, until it died later when the group was in the Mene Grande area, where the photo was taken. He also called De Loys a prankster and said Montandon was a bad person.

Q: What racist hypothesis of human evolution did a Swiss anthropologist use the De Loys photo to support?

A: George-Alexis Montandon was a Swiss anthropologist who, in the 1920s, latched onto the De Loys Ape photo (see previous entry for more details). Montandon was a proponent of a racist notion of the time called the "hologenesis hypothesis," which was a belief that humankind descended from different species of ape depending on geographic location. He believed that Asians descended from orangutans and that Africans descended from gorillas. And Montandon decided that the creature in the photo was a remnant of an unknown human ancestor he called *Ameranthropoides loysi*, a newly discovered ancestor of the native peoples of the American continents. The only evidence he presented was the De Loys photo. But, as the previous entry noted, the photograph wasn't of a continental "missing link" but of a propped-up, deceased spider monkey whose tail had been cut off. The hologenesis hypothesis was wishful-thinking racist bunk from Europeans who didn't seem to like the idea that they were part of the same evolutionary line as the rest of humanity.

Montandon also went on to write the anti-Semitic 1940 book *How to Recognize a Jew*, which was used by Nazi propagandists to inform a 1941 exhibition in Paris called "Le Juif et la France" ("The Jew and France") that included extremely anti-Semitic stereotypes and caricatures of Jewish people in the guise of science.

Q: What cryptozoologist founded the Society for the Investigation of the Unexplained?

A: Naturalist and early cryptozoologist Ivan T. Sanderson founded an organization called the Society for the Investigation of the Unexplained (SITU), dedicated to reports in the sciences of phenomena that couldn't be explained, including accounts of the paranormal and cryptozoological sightings. SITU would help field researchers in various ways, including providing advice and raising funds, and results were reviewed by a panel of twenty scientists and published in their journal *Pursuits*. That is, until the organization was shut down in the 1980s.

Q: What cryptozoologist founded and runs an organization for researching the Skunk Ape?

A: Dave Shealy, a cryptozoologist who studies the Skunk Ape of the Florida Everglades, started the Skunk Ape Research Headquarters in Ochopee, Florida. He believes there to be at least seven Skunk Apes living in the area. He reportedly sighted one himself when he was ten, which started him on this path, and he has had two more sightings since. Visitors to the center can purchase souvenirs, including the *Everglades Skunk Ape Research Field Guide*, and can even book a campsite on the premises from which to conduct their own field research.

Q: What cryptozoologist gained interest in the field after a childhood encounter with the Mogollon Monster?

A: In the 1940s, a thirteen-year-old boy on a Boy Scout camping trip in the Payson, Arizona, area reportedly awoke to a big, hairy hominid with a square-shaped head foraging for food at the campsite—none other than the Mogollon Monster (see Chapter Two for more info). The creature stood over the boy's sleeping bag before departing. The boy was Don Davis, who grew up to become a cryptozoologist.

Q: What cryptozoologist has written not one but three books about the Boggy Creek Monster of Arkansas?

A: Cryptozoologist Lyle Blackburn has written three books about the Boggy Creek Monster (see Chapter Two) of Fouke, Arkansas, also known as the Fouke Monster: *The Beast of Boggy Creek* (2012), *Beyond Boggy Creek* (2017), and *Boggy Creek Casebook* (2020).

Q: What book by ufologists was written about 1955 sightings?

A: Ufologists Isabel Davis and Ted Bloecher collaborated on a book called *Close Encounters at Kelly and Others of 1955*, about alleged alien and UFO sightings in 1955, including the case in Kelly, Kentucky, of the Hopkinsville Goblins (see Chapter Five for more info on that bizarre case).

Q: Who founded the Center for UFO Studies?

A: The Center for UFO Studies is a group founded in 1973 by astronomer Dr. J. Allen Hynek, who was one of the Project Blue Book civilian investigators (see Chapter Five for more on this government operation to study UFO sightings).

Q: What cryptozoologist spent several years in a gulag in Soviet Russia?

A: French-born cryptozoologist and surgeon Dr. Marie-Jeanne Koffmann spent much of her life in Russia. As were many people during the reign of Stalin, she was thrown into a gulag and kept there from 1948 to 1954 under suspicion of being a spy for France. Once released, she traveled as a doctor with an official Soviet expedition to the Pamir Mountains to study Almasty, often referred to by Russian researchers as the "Snowmen" or "Siberian Snowmen." She spent decades doing fieldwork to document accounts of the Almasty. Eventually moving back to France, she passed away there in 2021 at the ripe old age of 101!

Q: Who opened the International Cryptozoology Museum?

A: Loren Coleman is a famous American cryptozoologist who has done extensive fieldwork and written and cowritten dozens of books on the subject, including *Mysterious America* and *Bigfoot! The True Story of Apes in America*. In 2003, he opened the International Cryptozoology Museum in Portland, Maine, which you can still visit today. A new branch of the museum was opened in Bangor, Maine, in 2022, and an additional site was added in 2023. The newest location, an architectural Streamline Moderne building located at 490 Broadway, Bangor, will be expanded and renovated during 2023 and 2024.

Chapter 10

POP GOES THE SASQUATCH

CRYPTIDS IN LITERATURE, POP CULTURE, AND MEDIA

Q: What two famous works of English poetry reference the sea creature Fastitocalon?

A: The creature Fastitocalon, one of the versions of the aspidochelone, is referenced in two major works. The first is the Old English poem "The Whale," written by an unknown author in medieval times. The second is a poem entitled "Fastitocalon" in *The Adventures of Tom Bombadil*, a book of poetry by J. R. R. Tolkien (Tom Bombadil is a character from Tolkien's *The Fellowship of the Ring* from his Lord of the Rings series). Both poems are about sailors mistaking a giant sea creature for an island and drowning when the creature submerges. "The Whale," as the title would suggest, seems to describe a whale, while "Fastitocalon" describes a giant sea turtle of Middle Earth. The use of the same name is no wonder since Tolkien's Middle Earth mythology was heavily influenced by medieval works, including Old English literature and mythology.

Q: What cryptid did Alfred, Lord Tennyson write a poem about?

A: "The Kraken" is an unusually structured sonnet-like poem by Alfred, Lord Tennyson, released in 1830 in his book *Poems, Chiefly Lyrical*. It describes, as the name would suggest, the fearsome Kraken, slumbering in the depths of the ocean, but who, when the seas are heated by the end of the world, will rise to the surface and perish.

Q: What fierce one-horned creature was said to be gifted to Alexander the Great after he defeated a sea serpent?

A: Sometimes Alexander the Great's horse Bucephalus is depicted as having one horn. But that's not the only unicorn-like creature in his legends. In the thirteenth-century work

The Wonders of Creation by historian Zakarīyā Ibn Muḥammad al-Qazwīnī, it is said that Alexander killed a sea serpent that was plaguing the inhabitants of Jazirat al-Tinnin, an island in the Indian Ocean. He succeeded and was rewarded with an Al-mi'raj, described as a fierce creature that looked like a large yellow hare with a long black horn sticking out of the middle of its head (like a bunny unicorn).

Q: What sea serpent of biblical mythology was slain by God to feed the Hebrews?

A: The Leviathan, *Livyatan* in Hebrew, is an enormous multi-headed sea creature mentioned in the Old Testament of the Bible in multiple places, including in Psalm 74, which says that God broke the heads of Leviathan into pieces and gave him as meat to the people living in the wilderness. This is a reference to the forty-year period the Bible says the Israelites were doomed to wander the wilderness before settling in the Promised Land.

Q: What figure of Norse mythology transformed into a dragon due to his greed?

A: In the *Volsunga Saga,* an epic work of Norse mythology, Hreithmar is a man who received gold from Odin in compensation for the slaying of one of his sons. Another of his sons, Fafnir, slayed Hreithmar for the gold. Fafnir guarded the gold, and his greed transformed him into a dragon. The Norse hero Sigurd later slayed the dragon Fafnir.

Q: What classic 1950 film features a creature of Celtic folklore?

A: In the 1950 film *Harvey,* James Stewart plays Elwood P. Dowd, a man who hangs out with and has conversations with an invisible six-foot rabbit-like creature he calls Harvey that he explains is actually a pooka. In Celtic Irish folklore, a pooka (or púca) is a shape-shifting trickster that can appear as an animal or a human, and can talk, sometimes foretelling disaster.

Q: What cryptid is mentioned in the original 1954 *Godzilla* movie?

A: A scientist in the 1954 movie *Godzilla*, Dr. Kyohei Yamane, played by renowned Japanese actor Takashi Shimura, makes a speech in which he references the footprints of snowmen found in the Himalayas as an example of things existing that are still unknown to science. In the speech, he is addressing a group of officials and suggesting they launch an expedition to Odo Island for scientific research. This talk of the Himalayan snowmen is, of course, a reference to the Yeti.

Q: What mysterious cryptid did both John Steinbeck and his son write about?

A: John Steinbeck included a mention of the Dark Watchers (see Chapter Six for the eerie details) in his 1938 short story "Flight" in his book *The Long Valley*. And John Steinbeck's son, Thomas, heard tales of the creature growing up, prompting him to research them and write a nonfiction book called *In Search of the Dark Watchers* with artist Benjamin Brode, who visited Big Sur after Steinbeck told him about the cryptids and created a series of paintings for the book.

Q: What early zoological work also included cryptids?

A: Linguist, botanist, and naturalist Conrad Gesner, born in 1516 in Zurich, Switzerland, is considered the founder of zoology. From 1551 to 1558, he wrote a four-volume, roughly four-thousand-page work called the *Historiae animalium*, in which he sought to describe all known animals at the time, including woodcut illustrations of the creatures. Most were real animals, but some, especially in the fourth volume, were cryptids, like mermaids, unicorns, sea serpents, and even the Kraken of Norse mythology. Gesner died of plague in 1565, leaving behind much unfinished work.

Q: **Where did the legend of the vampire originate?**

A: We often think of vampires as originating in Romania with stories of Vlad Tepes (aka Vlad the Impaler), or with Irish author Bram Stoker's novel *Dracula*. But the word "vampire," or *vampir*, and the associated legends actually originated in Serbia in the 1720s. In fact, the novel *After Ninety Years,* by Milovan Glisic, about the legend of vampire Sava Savanovic and a related love story that unfolds around the cursed mill, was published in 1880, seventeen years before the novel *Dracula* came out in 1897. The 1973 movie *Leptirica*, based on Glisic's book, is considered the first Serbian horror film.

Q: **What sports teams have cryptid connections?**

A: In 1993, the New Jersey NHL hockey team retired their old mascot due to a fondling scandal, rebranded themselves the New Jersey Devils, and took on a red-horned devil mascot based on the Jersey Devil cryptid. He doesn't have wings, however, unless they are tucked under his hockey jersey. Here are a few other cryptid-branded teams:

- The Cleveland Monsters (formerly the Lake Erie Monsters), an AHL hockey team, has South Bay Bessie as their logo.

- The Vermont Lake Monsters baseball team has Champ, a Lake Champlain cryptid, as its mascot.
- The Seattle Kraken NHL hockey team is named for the Kraken cryptid.
- The Kelowna Rockets, a junior hockey team in Kelowna, British Columbia, Canada, who play in the Western Hockey League (WHL), have Ogopogo as their logo and mascot.

Q: **Which creature, once thought to be a cryptid but later scientifically recognized, inspired a major plot point in the 1933 film *King Kong*?**

A: Oddly enough, it wasn't just the scientific discovery of gorillas that inspired Merian C. Cooper to write the movie *King Kong* (released in 1933). It was also the large monitor lizard and former cryptid the Komodo dragon, recognized by scientists in 1912. An explorer friend of Cooper's, William Douglas Burden, was part of an expedition to Indonesia tasked with bringing back specimens. The group captured fifteen (thirteen dead and two live). The two live Komodo dragons were put on display in the Bronx Zoo. Also on display at the zoo was a taxidermied gorilla (there were no live ones in North America at the time) that was perhaps even more popular than the dragons. Sadly, with the New York climate and the zoo enclosure not being close to their natural habitat, and the zookeepers not knowing what to feed them, the two Komodo dragons died within two months of arrival at the zoo. Merian C. Cooper later wrote to Burden and stated that when Burden told him that the Komodo dragons had been killed by civilization, that led Cooper to have his gorilla protagonist meet the same fate.

Q: In what early Yeti film did a debate occur about whether an imported Yeti should be handled by customs or immigration?

A: In the 1954 movie *The Snow Creature* (likely the first feature film about the Himalayan Yeti), an expedition looking for plants instead encounters a group of Yetis. One is captured and brought back to Los Angeles, California, where amusingly, because the creature is listed as a "snowman" ("man" being the operative word), they can't decide whether it should be handled by customs or immigration. During the confusion, the Yeti of course escapes and wreaks havoc.

Q: What early Yeti-centered TV movie was remade into a feature film, both starring Peter Cushing?

A: In 1955, a TV movie called *The Creature* aired as part of the *BBC Sunday-Night Theatre* program in which a scientist (played by Peter Cushing) doing research in the Himalayas is talked into going on a Yeti hunt. The movie was remade in 1957 as the feature film *The Abominable Snowman*, with Peter Cushing reprising his role.

Q: What movie is known as the first film about Bigfoot?

A: *The Legend of Boggy Creek*, released in 1972, is a low-budget feature film directed by Arkansas filmmaker Charles B. Pierce, written by Earl E. Smith, and shot in a narrated documentary style. The film tells the story of the town's dealings with the Boggy Creek Monster, a Bigfoot-like creature said to roam the creeks around the Fouke, Arkansas, area (see Chapter Two for more details about this cryptid). Many locals who have had their own Boggy Creek Monster encounters played themselves in the movie. *The Legend of Boggy Creek* is often cited as the first feature film about a Bigfoot creature.

The film was followed by a 1983 sequel called *Boggy Creek II: And the Legend Continues*, which also appeared as an episode of the movie parody show *Mystery Science Theater 3000* on May 9, 1999.

Q: In what film does a Bigfoot creature terrorize people in the swamps of Louisiana?

A: In the 1976 film *Creature from Black Lake*, directed by Joy N. Houck, Jr., two grad students from the University of Chicago drive down to Oil City, Louisiana, in the hopes of proving the existence of Bigfoot.

Q: What popular car model bore the name of a cryptid?

A: In the 1950s, the Ford Motor Company decided to add a sporty car to their offerings. The first Ford Thunderbird was built in 1954 and zoomed into popularity. People often called it the T-Bird for short. Ford also developed a racing version that won over 150 NASCAR races over the years. This powerful vehicle bore the name of a powerful North American mythical creature, the thunderbird. The Ford Thunderbird ceased production in the mid 1990s with a special fiftieth anniversary model appearing in 2005.

Q: What British superhero TV show starring puppets bore the name of a cryptid?

A: *Thunderbirds* was a British show that ran from 1965 to 1966 about a billionaire family-run organization called International Rescue that, as the name would suggest, rescued people all over the world. The Thunderbirds in the series were the five advanced vehicles, aptly named Thunderbird 1 through Thunderbird 5, that enabled the team to travel through air, water, over land, and even into space to pull off the rescues. Also of note is that the characters were all marionette-style puppets with an electronically controlled lower lip for mouth movements.

Q: What movie erroneously put a twelfth century Norwegian mythological creature in an Ancient Greek setting?

A: The 1981 film *Clash of the Titans* gave us a tale of the hero Perseus (mortal son of Zeus) fighting to save his love interest Andromeda, while both aided and opposed by gods and goddesses of the Greek pantheon (including his dad Zeus, played by Lawrence Olivier). Perseus encounters enemies and allies along the way, including giant scorpions, the three Stygian witches, the fearsome gorgon Medusa (who had snakes for hair and turned men to stone with a glance), the winged steed Pegasus, and Bubo (a quirky animatronic metal owl made by Hephaestus). The film also gave us the iconic line, "Release the Kraken," referring to a sea creature to whom Andromeda is to be sacrificed.

But the Kraken wasn't a member of Ancient Greek mythology. Ancient Greece did have other sea creatures like Scylla, Charybdis, and the sirens. The Kraken is a creature of Norwegian origin, first described by King Sverre in the year 1180.

Q: In what 1980s film did a Sasquatch move in with a family?

A: The 1987 movie *Harry and the Hendersons* stars John Lithgow, Melinda Dillon, and the late Kevin Peter Hall (as

Harry). In the film, the titular family hits a Bigfoot with their car and, thinking he's dead, they bring him home, where he wakes up, of course. They call the creature Harry, and, thankfully, Harry is friendly, or the movie wouldn't have been a comedy. The film was also adapted into a sitcom that lasted from 1991 to 1993.

Q: What cryptid made an appearance in the movie *Big Trouble in Little China*?

A: The John Carpenter film *Big Trouble in Little China* incorporated a number of Chinese legends, including China's own Bigfoot-like cryptid, the Yeren. In the final scene when the good guys have prevailed and truck driver Jack Burton (played by Kurt Russell) drives off, a Yeren can be seen hitching a ride underneath his vehicle.

Q: What series on Animal Planet, premised on hunting for a famous hairy hominid, ran for seven years?

A: The premise of the Animal Planet series *Finding Bigfoot* was that investigators from the Bigfoot Field Researchers Organization would travel all over the US and the world in search of the elusive Bigfoot (and other Bigfoot-like creatures). The first episode, "Bigfoot Crossing in Georgia," aired on May 30, 2011, and the last, aptly entitled "The 100th Episode," aired on May 28, 2018. The researchers never found Bigfoot, but they had fun trying.

Q: What Japanese anime series features sea monsters?

A: The long-running Japanese animation TV show *One Piece* is set during the Great Age of Pirates when, after the death of the Pirate King and news that he left a great treasure called

One Piece hidden somewhere, lots of people became pirates and set to the seas in search of the treasure. One such lad is the main character, a teenager named Luffy. And one of the things the seafaring cast of the show encounter is the occasional sea serpent. *One Piece* first aired in 1999 and is still going, having amassed over one thousand episodes!

Q: **What California- and Nevada-dwelling cryptid is the title character of a children's book?**

A: Bob McCormick wrote a fictional children's book called *The Story of Tahoe Tessie: The Original Lake Tahoe Monster* about the history of Lake Tahoe and how Tessie came to dwell there. It was published in 1985. The author also wore a dinosaur-like Tessie costume to local events.

Q: **What West Virginia cryptids are featured in the video game *Fallout 76*?**

A: In the video game *Fallout 76*, set in the Appalachian hills of West Virginia after a nuclear apocalypse, a number of cryptids roam the countryside, giving grief to players. There is a cult of non-player characters who worship the Mothman, a West Virginia cryptid who was sighted in the Point Pleasant area in the 1960s. The Mothman is supposed to be fearsome and deadly, but a harmless "wise Mothman" materializes during the event "The Path to Enlightenment." But that's not the only local cryptid who made it into the game. The Flatwoods Monster also makes rare appearances, although it is presented as an alien in a hovering suit of armor with a domed helmet and purple, glowing eyes. The Grafton Monster wanders a dry riverbed in the town of Charleston, West Virginia, and appears in events in Grafton and other locations in the game.

And *Fallout 76* also features the Sheepsquatch, the Snallygaster, and the Wendigo (which are all quite deadly in the game).

Q: What movie was based on the Mokele-Mbembe cryptid legends?

A: The 1985 movie *Baby: Secret of the Lost Legend*, starring Sean Young, William Katt, and Patrick McGoohan, involves scientists discovering a living brontosaurus family living on the Ivory Coast in Africa.

Q: What US cryptid had a musical written about it?

A: *Hot Damn! It's the Loveland Frog!* by Ohioans Mike Hall and Joshua Steele debuted at the Cincinnati Fringe Festival on May 29, 2014. The bluegrass musical told the story of someone trying to rescue a relative who had apparently been captured by a Loveland Frogman. It ran for five sold-out shows.

Q: What Great Lakes Brewing Company beer is named after a cryptid?

A: The Great Lakes Brewing Company produced a pale ale called Lake Erie Monster after the area's famous lake-dwelling cryptid, Bessie.

Q: What cryptid appears in a *CatDog* TV movie?

A: In the *CatDog* TV movie "CatDog and the Great Parent Mystery," which first aired November 25, 2000, on Nickelodeon, Lake Erie's own sea monster, Bessie, shows up and swallows CatDog! Fortunately, they are able to fashion a hairball to get themselves expelled.

Q: What five-star hotel is named after a cryptid?

A: Yak & Yeti is a five-star hotel in the city of Kathmandu, the capital of Nepal. It is, of course, partially named for the famous hairy bipedal cryptid of the area's Himalayan mountains, the Yeti. A restaurant named for the hotel is located in the Animal Kingdom Theme Park in Disney World in Orlando, Florida.

Q: What airline is named for a cryptid?

A: Yeti Airlines is the official airline of the country of Nepal.

Q: What cryptid appears in a famous animated Christmas movie?

A: The 1964 classic *Rudolph the Red-Nosed Reindeer* has many fanciful characters of legend, like Santa Claus, his elf helpers, and his flying reindeer. But another costar of the stop-motion cartoon is the famous Himalayan cryptid, the Yeti! He's referred to as the Abominable Snow Monster (or Bumble, for short), and as usual in pop-culture appearances, he has white fur (see Chapter Two for the Yeti's hair color in sighting accounts).

Q: What amusement park ride features the Yeti as the antagonist?

A: The Expedition Everest ride at the Animal Kingdom Theme Park in Disney World in Orlando, Florida, opened in 2006. The queue takes "explorers" through a museum of Yeti artifacts and a Tibetan tour office. And then on to the train, where you are menaced by a giant Yeti!

Another fun fact: Like Mount Everest is the tallest peak in the world, Expedition Everest is the tallest roller-coaster at any Disney Park to date.

Q: In what popular video game does a hairy hominid wander an open-world dig site to learn about humans?

A: The Nintendo game *A Monster's Expedition* features a Sasquatch-like creature who you take on a journey around a set of tiny islands. You have to solve a puzzle of how to create a tree bridge or raft to the next island. Many of the little islands feature exhibits of human artifacts with amusing possible explanations, such as a postcard with a plaque reading "Holidaying humans liked to send pictures they didn't take to people they didn't like, claiming that they wished those other humans were present."

Q: What Bigfoot-branded product will keep you up at night?

A: Coffee company Majestic Blends was born of the Pacific Northwest—just like Bigfoot. One of their signature coffees is their Bigfoot Dark Roast. The ubiquitous hairy hominid even appears on their packaging.

Q: In what Pixar film does the Yeti have a cameo?

A: In the 2001 Pixar animated film *Monsters Inc.*, a large white-furred Yeti (voiced by John Ratzenberger) makes an appearance when main characters Mike and Sully end up in the Himalayas. The Yeti offers them snow cones, complains about his "abominable" nickname, and even references his buddy Bigfoot!

Q: In what 2017 film do plane crash survivors encounter a Yeren?

A: In the 2017 film *Journey to the Forbidden Valley*, a plane crash-lands in a remote part of China, where the survivors encounter the fabled hairy hominid the Yeren and have to thwart poachers after the cryptid.

Q: What famous brand of cooler is named after a cryptid?

A: A brand of high-quality (and high-priced) coolers launched in 2006 by a pair of outdoorsman brothers who were frustrated with how breakable all the available coolers seemed to be. They called the company YETI, like the cold-weather Himalayan cryptid.

Q: In what episode of *The Simpsons* is Homer mistaken for Bigfoot?

A: In season 1, episode 7 of the long-running animated series *The Simpsons* called "The Call of the Simpsons," the family goes camping after buying a junker RV. They narrowly escape when Homer drives it over a cliff. Marge and Lisa set up camp while Homer and Bart wander into the woods to look for help (with Maggie following them and having her own side adventure with a family of bears). Homer and Bart lose their clothing after falling down a waterfall. They cover their loins with foliage. Homer eats honey out of a beehive and is stung, rendering himself unable to talk intelligibly. He runs and falls into a muddy creek, where he is filmed by a naturalist shooting a video. Homer immediately makes the news as the legendary Bigfoot, and hilarity ensues.

Q: What snack company ran a series of ads featuring Sasquatch?

A: Food company Jack Link's, which sells beef jerky and related snacks (as well as some merchandise featuring

Sasquatch), produced a series of commercials dubbed "Messin' with Sasquatch" to promote its beef jerky. In the ads, people (usually campers) would play a practical joke on Sasquatch and then get their comeuppance.

Q: In what animated TV episode does someone shave Sasquatch to pass him off as human?

A: In "Home Insecurity," season 1, episode 3 of the animated series The Venture Bros., Brock Samson goes camping in an area where a military operation is underway. He comes upon a Sasquatch, who he proceeds to fight until Steve Summers (a parody of the Bionic Man) steps in to save the beast. It turns out that Steve fled into the woods from conscription into government service (which they expected him to do to pay off the six-million-dollars' worth of new body parts). There he happened upon Sasquatch and fell in love. Brock helps the pair escape, and Steve states that they'll probably head to Canada, where Sasquatch has relatives. And this isn't the first time a bionic man has encountered Bigfoot. In the show *The Six Million Dollar Man*, Steve Austin (the astronaut Steve Summers is a parody of) encounters large Bigfoot-like creatures in "The Secret of Bigfoot," which aired in two parts in February 1976.

Q: In what animated TV episode does a scientist state that the Chupacabra does not exist, only to ultimately be attacked by a Chupacabra?

A: In *The Venture Bros.* season 1, episode 1, called "Dia de los Dangerous," scientist Doctor Venture takes his two sons and their bodyguard Brock Samson to Tijuana, Mexico. Venture is a guest lecturer at a university where he states that "the myth of the Chupacabra is utter crap." Later in the episode, a creature with claws and red, glowing eyes jumps out of Brock's car and attacks Doctor Venture. Brock kills it. When Doctor Venture asks what it was, Brock says, "Chupacabra. They're all over Mexico."

Q: What '80s metal song is about a hairy hominid?

A: The song "Big Foot" by the band Alcatrazz, on their 1983 album *No Parole from Rock 'N' Roll*, sounds like it would be about the hairy hominid of the US Pacific Northwest, Bigfoot. But it refers to a creature in the snowy Himalayan mountains, which is obviously the Yeti.

Q: In what animated series did the Hodag appear?

A: Wisconsin's Hodag appeared in the animated TV episode *Scooby-Doo! Mystery Incorporated*, season 2, episode 5, "The Hodag of Horror," which aired August 3, 2012. A vehicle called the Traveling Cabinet of Curiosities comes into Crystal Cove ("the most hauntedest place on earth," according to the town sign). Scooby and Shaggy visit the exhibits and see the Hodag on display. They decide that it looks fake, until it starts attacking people and stealing their jewelry. But the Scooby gang is on the case and unmasks the real bad guy.

Q: In what found-footage documentary-style movie does a film crew hunt for the Jersey Devil?

A: In the film *The Last Broadcast*, released in 1998, a narrator walks the audience through the evidence in a mystery called "The Jersey Devil Murders." Much of the evidence is footage shot by the crew of a fictitious public-access show called *Fact or Fiction*, shot when the showrunners took an online chat suggestion to do a show about the Jersey Devil (see Chapter

Five for more information on this local cryptid). The crew decides to do a live simulcast on the public-access channel and on the web, and they enlist help. The mockumentary reveals at the beginning that two of the crew were found viciously murdered, and all that remained of another was a cap and blood on the snow. The narrator slowly reveals pieces of the mystery using segments of fourteen hours of unaired found footage, newspaper articles, news broadcasts, interviews with people who knew the crew or were involved with the case, and interviews with a woman working to restore damaged footage to determine who, or what, was really to blame for the murders.

Q: In what movie does Sherlock Holmes mention one cryptid and encounter another?

A: In *The Private Life of Sherlock Holmes* (1970), written and directed by Billy Wilder, Sherlock Holmes (played by Robert Stephens) and his partner in crime-solving Dr. Watson (played by Colin Blakely) are embroiled in a case where one cryptid is mentioned briefly and another plays a key role in the plot.

Holmes is tasked with investigating the disappearance of a Belgian woman's husband, an engineer.

In a scene at the Diogenes Club, while talking to his brother Mycroft Holmes (played by Christopher Lee) about the case, Sherlock Holmes mentions an expedition to the Himalayas that was ostensibly to search for the Yeti.

But the Yeti isn't the most relevant cryptid. The case of the missing man takes Holmes and Watson to Inverness, Scotland, and directly to Loch Ness. They happen upon three graves being covered in dirt, and the grave digger tells them he believes the Loch Ness Monster was responsible for the deaths of the three people, who were pulled from the water, reportedly after their boat tipped over, and looking like they were scared to death. Later, Watson even spots Nessie!

But as you would expect in a mystery, everything is not as it seems, and Holmes and Watson soon uncover the truth about the creature.

In an interesting bit of related news, the model of the supposed monster used in the movie was found at the bottom of Loch Ness in 2016! Norwegian company Kongsberg Maritime used a robot to capture pictures of the thirty-foot model.

Q: What Marvel comics hero had the form of a hairy hominid cryptid?

A: Marvel character Walter Langkowski, a Canadian who was both a pro football player and an MIT-educated scientist, became a Marvel superhero named Sasquatch. Walter exposed himself to gamma radiation hoping to transform like the Hulk. He did transform, but unbeknownst to him, it was by breaking open a mystical barrier that let the Great Beast Tanaraq through, causing Walter to take his orange-haired ten-foot-tall Sasquatch-like form. Sasquatch became a member of Canadian superhero team Alpha Flight. The character made his first appearance in 1979 in *Uncanny X-Men* #120. Later he battled a Marvel incarnation of another cryptid: Wendigo.

Q: In what cartoon episode does a miniature golf course feature cryptids?

A: In *Bob's Burgers* season 13, episode 8, "Putts-giving," which aired November 20, 2022, the Belchers realize on Thanksgiving that their 50 percent-off coupon to Mystery Planet World Mini-Golf expires that day. The kids convince their parents to take them to the golf course, where Louis and Gene manage to break the dancing Yeti, a white, hairy Yeti creature affixed to model snowcapped mountains and whose legs swing over one of the holes, doing different movements depending upon which of three holes a golf ball is putted through. They spend the rest of the episode trying to fix it before the manager or their parents find out. And although the Yeti is the most prominent cryptid, it is not the only one featured in the episode. You see a host of creatures in the background, including little green aliens, a mermaid, and a sea serpent.

Q: What cryptid is the song "The Legend" by DJ Steve Cook about?

A: In 1987, Michigan DJ Steve Cook of WTCM radio recorded and released a song called "The Legend" about the Michigan Dogman. This song later inspired Mike Agrusa to create fake video evidence of the cryptid, which was posted by Cook on his website as proof of the existence of the Dogman (see Chapter Eight for more details of the hoax).

Q: What 2012 movie featured a famous Michigan cryptid?

A: In the movie *Dogman*, written and directed by Richard Brauer and released to video in 2012, a couple who live in a rural area have noticed things are going missing, including their chickens. Soon, sightings and attacks begin, where the perpetrator is described as a big dog with glowing yellow eyes that stands on his hind legs. The culprit is the Michigan Dogman! The movie even features a clip of the famous "Gable Film" (see just above, and also Chapter Eight, "Faking It: Famous Hoaxes," for more information on the clip, and

Chapter Five, "A Bit of Americana: Regional Cryptids of the US," for more info on the Michigan Dogman).

Q: In what board game are players cryptozoologists on the trail of an unclassified animal?

A: Cryptid is a modular board game designed by Hal Duncan and Ruth Veevers and illustrated by Kwanchai Moriya. In the game, players are cryptozoologists trying to piece together clues on the whereabouts of a cryptid, but also trying to misdirect the other cryptozoologists to throw them off the track.

Q: What movie relocates a South Dakota cryptid to Tennessee?

A: *Taku-He*, written and directed by George Demick and released in 2017, is named for the Bigfoot-like South Dakota creature. Because the production company is located in Tennessee, the monster is relocated to Riverdale, Tennessee. In the film, a production company is scouting the area for a zombie film. A couple whose farm they agree to use as a location tell them about a creature that comes out at night, circles their property, and even carried off one of their cows. Among each other, one of the film crew mentions the Fouke Monster and the 1972 movie *The Legend of Boggy Creek*, and later, the 1976 Bigfoot movie *Creature from Black Lake*. The producer convinces the investors to provide extra cash for the crew to also shoot a documentary about the creature. They interview locals about what they call the Riverdale Monster, and then camp in the woods for their own encounter.

Q: What American cryptids appear in the 2017 edition of the book *Fantastic Beasts and Where to Find Them*?

A: There are, of course, both ancient mythological and completely made-up creatures in the wizarding world of *Harry Potter*, and especially in its sister franchise *Fantastic Beasts and Where to Find Them*. The original pre-movie *Fantastic Beasts and Where to Find Them* book by J. K. Rowling came out in 2001, but in 2017 a new edition was released, and it included six new animals—and all of them are from American folklore. These include the Hidebehind, the Hodag, the Horned Serpent, the Snallygaster, the thunderbird, and the Wampus cat (see Chapters Three, Four, Five, Six, and Eight for more information on these fantastic beasts).

Q: What fictitious character of the US West was said to have encountered a hoop snake?

A: In the many adventures of Pecos Bill, a larger-than-life Texas cowboy character created by journalist Edward "Tex" O'Reilly (with some stories written by others), one of the dangers he evaded was the deadly hoop snake (see Chapter Six, "World Wide What?!?: Miscellaneous Cryptids the World Over," for more info on the hoop snake).

Q: What beloved 1960s animated series featured a kid and his sea serpent friend?

A: The series *Beany and Cecil*, created by Bob Clampett of Looney Tunes fame, starred a kid named Beany and his sea serpent friend Cecil, who had the rather unfortunate affliction of sea-sickness. The series aired in 1962.

Q: What 1970s show starred a sea monster and his human friends?

A: The Sid and Marty Krofft live-action show *Sigmund and the Sea Monsters* ran for two seasons from 1973 to 1975. In the show, a young sea monster named Sigmund runs away from his sea monster family and befriends two human boys, Johnny and Scott.

Q: What Jane Austen mash-up novel featured cryptids?

A: *Sense and Sensibility and Sea Monsters* is a 2009 book by Ben H. Winters (and Jane Austen) that is a reimagining of Jane Austen's *Sense and Sensibility*. In the novel, the Dashwoods not only have to deal with the death of their patriarch and navigate society after a lowering of their financial and social status, but they also have to battle sea monsters!

Q: In what *X-Files* episodes do Mulder and Scully investigate apparent cryptids?

A: The team of FBI agents on the show *The X-Files* (which ran from 1993 to 2001, with added seasons in 2016 and 2018) are tasked with investigating cases that seem to be in the extraterrestrial or paranormal realm. Agent Fox Mulder is the true believer, and his partner Agent Dana Scully is the science-minded skeptic. And sometimes their cases involved cryptids. Here are a few episodes where the pair acted as cryptozoologists:

- "The Jersey Devil," season 1, episode 5, first aired October 8, 1993: The team investigates a murder where the suspect is—you guessed it—the Jersey Devil.
- "Quagmire," season 3, episode 22, first aired May 3, 1996: The pair head to rural Georgia where a lake

monster rather like Nessie, but called Big Blue, is suspected of a couple of disappearances. As a bonus, the creature is said to inhabit Heuvelmans Lake (no doubt named for the famed "father of cryptozoology," Bernard Heuvelmans).

o "El Mundo Gira," season 4, episode 11, first aired January 12, 1997: Mulder and Scully investigate a murder that locals believe to be the work of a Chupacabra, although the team suspects otherwise.

Q: What cryptid is potentially referenced in the 1973 George Lucas film, *American Graffiti*?

A: In *American Graffiti*, the 1973 film directed and co-written by George Lucas, Terry, aka Toad (played by Charles Martin Smith) has borrowed his friend Steve's (Ron Howard) hotrod and parks with Debbie (Candy Clark). They exit the vehicle and someone steals the car, leaving them to walk on a secluded road in the woods alone. They hear noises, and Debbie says maybe it's the goat killer, and explains that a murderer is leaving goat heads by his victims. Then we hear the sound of a goat, and the two hide. The film is set in the 1950s and was made in the 1970s, both times when the Maryland Goatman was in the news, so it's not out of the question that the "goat killer" was a modified Goatman reference. Urban legends morph over time, and in one iteration of the legend, the Goatman goes after teenagers (including teens parked at Lover's Lanes) to avenge his goats who were killed by a teen prank.

Q: What gory movie features the Maryland Goatman as its antagonist?

A: *Deadly Detour: The Goat Man Murders*, directed by Mike O'Mahony and released in 2011, is a microbudget gross-out gore-fest where young people (including a group who stop in Maryland on their way to Florida) are picked off by a killer known as the Goat Man.

Q: What sitcom featured a pigman cryptid?

A: In the popular sitcom *Seinfeld*, season 5, episode 5, entitled "The Bris," one of the running stories involves Kramer seeing a pigman in a room at the hospital (the audience sees his reaction and hears pig noises). The rest of the group doesn't believe him, but he's certain the hospital is somehow involved in a military plot to create an army of pigmen, which he says has been in the works since the 1950s (a likely reference to the Northfield Pigman reportedly spotted in 1951—see Chapter Five for more details). Kramer takes Jerry back to the hospital to prove it, but the room is empty. However, at the end of the episode, Kramer can be seen in the background being chased by hospital staff carrying an oinking pigman piggyback.

Q: What SyFy channel movie features a Wisconsin werewolf cryptid?

A: *The Beast of Bray Road*, directed by Leigh Scott and released in 2005, is about the Elkhorn, Wisconsin, cryptid of the same name (see Chapter Five). A new sheriff has to contend with a series of grizzly deaths that increasingly seem to be the work of a wolf-man, and a cryptozoologist shows up to lend a hand.

Q: What feel-good holiday movie re-creates famous cryptid footage?

A: The 2003 film *Elf* directed by Jon Favreau includes a scene where news footage shows Buddy the elf (Will Farrell) walking through the woods of Central Park. The footage bears a hilariously striking resemblance to the famous Gimlin and Patterson Bigfoot footage (see Chapter Two).

Q: **What mine-dwelling cryptid got its own movie in 2022?**

A: In the 2022 film *Night of the Tommyknockers*, directed by Michael Su and set in the 1800s during the Gold Rush, miners in Nevada dig too deep and unleash the Tommyknockers just before a band of outlaws comes to town to rob the bank of its gold. These movie monsters bear little resemblance to the descriptions of the cryptid in Chapter Six, but the opening scene makes mention of the folklore. The film was funded by an Indiegogo crowdfunding campaign.

Q: **What famous 1980s rock song makes an oblique reference to a famous monster?**

A: The song "Synchronicity II," on the 1983 *Synchronicity* album by The Police, tells the story of a man with a thankless job and home life. It parallels his angst with something emerging from a dark Scottish lake many miles away (the Loch Ness Monster).

CONCLUSION

Whether real or imaginary, cryptids are a fascinating subject. They range from mundane animals that could exist to fantastical creatures with mystical powers—and sometimes accessories like wands and top hats!

Some of us are exposed to the idea of cryptids early on, as parents use tales of all sorts of creatures to frighten children into obedience lest one of many bogeymen get them. And there is no shortage of mythology and urban legends and books, TV shows, and movies that reference cryptids and other monsters.

For many of these cryptids, there are multiple people who swear they've seen them. Perhaps many are cases of mistaken animal identity (bears standing on their hind legs and owls flying at frightened people and such), or tricks of the mind like pareidolia, mass hysteria, or the power of suggestion—legends brought to life by the human imagination.

Some of these myths and legends may have even been passed down orally from generation to generation from ancestors who actually shared the earth with hairy hominids, giant sloths, and all sorts of other creatures that don't exist anymore but once did.

Whatever you think of the topic, it is truly fascinating that every continent and a lot of local areas within those continents seem to have their own Sasquatch or Yeti-like ape-man creatures, most described remarkably similarly. Whether spirits that protect the forest, ancestral memories, psycho-logical or visual tricks our brains play on us, or real, living, breathing creatures that walk the earth, these phenomena make it seem like a small world after all.

It is also notable how many stories there are of people encountering what they believe are fantastic, unknown beasts immediately try to shoot them! Please, if you see a creature you don't recognize, shoot it with a camera, not a gun.

And if you go monster hunting, take a buddy, and of course use the sort of caution you'd use in any wild, natural setting. Because even if you don't find Bigfoot, there are bears and mountain lions and other predators out there, not to mention cliffs. And as '80s movies would have us believe, quicksand galore.

But we do hope you find Bigfoot.

REFERENCES

"6 of the Most Audacious Science Hoaxes Ever." *National Geographic*. February 12, 2015. https://www.nationalgeographic.com/history /article/150211-science-hoaxes-history.

"15 Kraken Facts and Myths to Release in Your Next Conversation." MentalFloss. Last updated January 1, 2020. https://www.mentalfloss .com/article/67371/15-kraken-facts-and-myths-unleash-conversation.

"61. Chacoan Peccary." Edge of Existence. Accessed November 10, 2022. http://www.edgeofexistence.org/species/chacoan-peccary.

"About the Bigfoot Field Researchers Organization (BFRO)." BFRO.net. Accessed November 9. 2022. https://www.bfro.net/REF/aboutbfr .asp.

Adams, Lee. "Securing Funding for the Original King Kong Was Almost as Impressive as the Film Itself." SlashFilm. May 10, 2022. https:// www.slashfilm.com/858593/securing-funding-for-the-original-king -kong-was-almost-as-impressive-as-the-film-itself.

"Advertising/Messin' with Sasquatch." TV Tropes. Accessed November 11, 2022. https://tvtropes.org/pmwiki/pmwiki.php/Advertising /MessinWithSasquatch.

"Ahuitzotl." *Encyclopedia Britannica*. January 1, 2022. https://www .britannica.com/biography/Ahuitzotl.

Akana, Kalani. "The Menehune: A True Race of People." *Ka Wai Ola News*. June 1, 2022. https://kawaiola.news/ka-naauao-o-na-kupuna /the-menehune-a-true-race-of-people.

Alberty, Michael. "Is There a Mysterious Monster Lurking in a Kansas Sinkhole?" *Kansas City*. July 10, 2020. https://kansascitymag.com /news/only-in-kc/is-there-a-mysterious-monster-lurking-in-a-kansas -sinkhole.

Anderson, Bethany. "The Legendary Altamaha Monster Wasn't Found Off the Georgia Coast; Here's Why It Was a Hoax." *First Coast News*. Last updated March 30, 2018. https://www.firstcoastnews.com/amp /article/news/local/georgia/the-legendary-altamaha-monster-wasnt -found-off-the-georgia-coast-heres-why-its-a-hoax/77-533319231.

Anderson, Dereck, and Joel Anderson. "Mythical Creatures: Ya-Te-Veo."
Anderson Design Group. Accessed October 16, 2022. https://www
.andersondesigngroupstore.com/a/collections/world-travel/mythical
-creatures-ya-te-veo.

Anderson Gerry, and Sylvia Anderson, created by. *Thunderbirds*. ITV
Network, 1965–1966.

Andrews, Evan. "The Cardiff Giant Fools the Nation, 145 Years Ago."
History. Last updated August 22, 2018. https://www.history.com
/news/the-cardiff-giant-fools-the-nation-145-yearsago.

Archer, Wesley, dir. *The Simpsons*. Season 1, Episode 7, "The Call of the
Simpsons." Aired February 18, 19910, Fox Network.

Atara, Pragati. "The Legend of The Phoenix–Is It All Just Folklore?"
Procaffenation. August 15, 2020. https://procaffenation.com
/phoenix-legends-did-they-ever-exist.

Austen, Jane, and Ben H. Winters. *Sense and Sensibility and Sea
Monsters*. Philadelphia: Quirk Books, 2009.

Avalos, Stefan, and Lance Weiler, dirs. *The Last Broadcast*. New Jersey:
FFM Productions, 1998.

Balasundaram, Nemesha. "The Loch Ness Legend: Eight Facts About the
Monster and the Salford-Irish Man Behind the Mystery." *Irish Post*.
April 14, 2016. https://www.irishpost.com/life-style/loch-ness
-monster-eight-fascinating-facts-about-the-salford-irish-man-behind
-the-hoax-86294.

"Basque." *Encyclopedia Britannica*. September 16, 2022. https://www
.britannica.com/topic/Basque.

"Beast of Exmoor." TheNationalParanormalSociety.org. January 19,
2022. http://national-paranormal-society.org/beast-exmoor.

"The Beginnings of Cryptozoology." Indiana University Bloomington.
January 23, 2021. https://blogs.iu.edu/sciu/2021/01/23/the
-beginnings-of-cryptozoology.

Bendici, Ray. "The Glawackus, Glastonbury." Damned Connecticut.
Accessed November 19, 2022. https://www.damnedct.com/the
-glawackus-glastonbury.

Benedict, Adam. "Cryptid Profile: Queensland Tiger." The Pine Barrens
Institute. August 18, 2018. https://pinebarrensinstitute.com
/cryptids/2018/8/18/cryptid-profile-queensland-tiger?format=amp.

"Bernard Heuvelmans: Father of Cryptozoology." BookBrowse.com. Accessed November 6, 2022. https://www.bookbrowse.com/mag /btb/index.cfm/book_number/3396/the-invisible-guardian.

"Beware the Bunyip." World Book. Accessed September 18, 2022. https://www.worldbook.com.au/bunyip.

"Beware the Legendary Best of 'Busco in Ind. Town." *Aiken Standard*. Last updated August 20, 2020. https://www.postandcourier.com /aikenstandard/news/beware-the-legendary-best-of-busco-in-ind -town/article_a7755a99-d236-59d1-bc02-ee48ae0ef361.html.

"Bigfoot Hoaxers Say It Was Just 'A Big Joke.'" CNN. August 21, 2008. https://edition.cnn.com/2008/US/08/21/bigfoot.hoax/#.

"Big Foot Lyrics." MetalKingdom.net. Accessed November 12, 2022. https://www.metalkingdom.net/lyrics-song/alcatrazz-big-foot -31797.

Bills, John William. "Serbia: The Birthplace of Vampires." Culture Trip. January 31, 2018. https://theculturetrip.com/europe/serbia/articles /serbia-birthplace-vampires/?amp=1.

"Biography–Oberon Zell." OberonZell.com. Accessed November 9, 2022. https://oberonzell.com/biography.

Black, Annetta. "Historiae Animalium." Odd Salon. April 26, 2017. https://oddsalon.com/historiae-animalium.

Black, Riley. "The Demise of the Komodo Kings." *National Geographic*. December 8, 2011. https://www.nationalgeographic.com/science /article/the-demise-of-the-komodo-kings.

Blackburn, Lyle. "About the Fouke Monster..." FoukeMonster.net. Accessed November 15, 2022. http://www.foukemonster.net.

Blakemore, Erin. "Aboriginal Australians." *National Geographic*. January 31, 2019. https://www.nationalgeographic.com/culture/article /aboriginal-australians.

Blitz, Matt. "The Goatman—Or His Story at Least—Still Haunts Prince George's County." *Washingtonian*. October 30, 2015. https://www .washingtonian.com/2015/10/30/the-goatman-or-his-story-at-least -still-haunts-prince-georges-county.

"Born in the Pacific Northwest." MajesticBlends.com. Accessed November 10, 2022. https://majesticblends.com/pages/story.

Braden, Beth. "10 Mountain Monsters Found Lurking in Appalachia." Travel Channel. Accessed October 8, 2022. https://www.travelchannel .com/shows/mountain-monsters/articles/10-mountain-monsters -found-lurking-in-appalachia.

Brauer, Richard. *Dogman*. Traverse City, MI: Brauer Productions Inc., 2012.

Breedlove, Seth, dir. *The Mothman Legacy*. Wadsworth, OH: Small Town Monsters, 2020.

Bressan, David. "De Loys' Ape Was a Well Played Anthropological Fraud." *Forbes*. January 31, 2016. https://www.forbes.com/sites /davidbressan/2016/01/31/de-loys-ape-was-a-well-played -anthropological-fraud/amp.

"Brigham Young." *History*. September 15, 2021. https://www.history .com/topics/religion/brigham-young.

Brown, Jordan D. "New Species Alert: Scientists Discover Giant Deep -Sea Isopod Family in Gulf of Mexico." *USA Today*. Last updated August 11, 2022. https://www.usatoday.com/story/news/nation /2022/08/11/new-species-giant-deep-sea-isopod-gulf-mexico /10285830002.

Brown, Julie. "'There's Something Out There': The Enduring Legend of Tahoe Tessie." *SF Gate*. May 4, 2021. https://www.sfgate.com /renotahoe/article/050521-lake-tahoe-tessie-monster-myths -16150906.php.

"Bunyip." *Britannica*. October 19, 2021. https://www.britannica .com/topic/bunyip.

"The Cape Ann Sea Serpent." HistoricIpswich.org. Accessed June 25, 2022. https://historicipswich.org/2019/03/26/cape-ann-sea -serpent.

Casey, Leo. "The Irish Legend of the Pooka." IrishCentral.com. Last updated December 4, 2022. https://www.irishcentral.com/roots /history/irish-legend-pooka.

Castelow, Ellen. "Spring Heeled Jack." *Historic UK*. Accessed November 12, 2022. https://www.historic-uk.com/CultureUK/Spring-Heeled -Jack.

"Chacoan Peccary." WCS Paraguay. Accessed November 10, 2022. https://paraguay.wcs.org/en-us/Wildlife/Chacoan-peccary.aspx.

"Champ, the Lake Champlain Monster." LakeChamplainRegion.com. Accessed October 19, 2022. https://www.lakechamplainregion.com /heritage/champ.

Chen, Laurie, Lea Li, and Jarrod Watt. "Inside China: In Search of the Yeren, The Chinese Bigfoot." *South China Morning Post*. August 24, 2018. SoundCloud. 14:41 minutes. https://m.soundcloud.com/south

-china-morning-post/inside-china-in-search-of-the-yeren-the
-wildman-of-china.

Cherones, Tom, dir. *Seinfeld*. Season 5, Episode 5, "The Bris." Aired
October 14, 1993. NBC.

"The Chimeric Missourium and Hydrarchos." ExtinctMonsters.net.
October 16, 2013. https://extinctmonsters.net/2013/10/16/the
-chimeric-missourium-and-hydrarchos.

"Chines Giant Salamander (Andrias davidianus)." San Diego Zoo
Wildlife Alliance. Accessed November 27, 2022. https://animals
.sandiegozoo.org/animals/chinese-giant-salamander.

Chong, Simon, dir. *Bob's Burgers*. Season 13, episode 8, "Putts-giving."
Aired November 20, 2022, FOX.

Clark, Jordan. "AMOMONGO: Visayan Folkloric Being or Cryptid?" The
Aswan Project. September 12, 2020. https://www.aswangproject
.com/amomongo.

Coleman, Loren. "Almasty Researcher Marie-Jeanne Koffmann,
101, Dies." Cryptozoonews.com. July 12, 2021. http://www
.cryptozoonews.com/mjkoffmann-obit.

Coleman, Loren. "The Meaning of Cryptozoology—Who Invented
the Term Cryptozoology?" International Cryptozoology Museum.
Accessed March 5, 2023. https://cryptozoologymuseum.com/what
-is-cryptozoology.

Coleman, Loren. "Taku-He and Cows in South Dakota." Cryptomundo.
com. September 7, 2007. http://cryptomundo.com/cryptozoo-news
/taku-he.

Coleman, Loren, and Jerome Clark. *Crypto-zoology A to Z: The
Encyclopedia of Loch Monsters, Sasquatch, Chupacabras, and Other
Authentic Mysteries of Nature*. New York: Touchstone, 2013.

Coleman, Loren, and Patrick Huyghe. *The Field Guide to Bigfoot, Yeti,
and Other Mystery Primates Worldwide*. New York: Avon Books, 1999.

Conway, John C.M. Koseman, and Darren Naish. *Cryptozoologicon:
The Biology, Evolution, and Mythology of Hidden Animals–Volume 1*.
Irregular Books: 2013.

Courage, Katherine Harmon. "Could an Octopus Really Be Terrorizing
Oklahoma's Lakes?" ScientificAmerican.com. December 19, 2013.
https://blogs.scientificamerican.com/octopus-chronicles/could-an
-octopus-really-be-terrorizing-oklahomae28099s-lakes.

Crair, Ben. "Why Do So Many People Still Want to Believe in Bigfoot?" *Smithsonian Magazine*. September 2018. https://www.smithsonianmag.com/history/why-so-many-people-still-believe-in-bigfoot-180970045.

Cartier, Rudolph, dir. *The Creature*. London, UK: BBC, 1955.

Crider, Beverly. "Hoop Snakes: Fact or Fiction?" Advance Local. Last updated April 13, 2012. https://www.al.com/strange-alabama/2012/04/hoop_snakes_are_no_hula_hoops.html.

Crosland Jr., Alan, dir. *The Six Million Dollar Man*. Season 3, episode 17, "The Secret of Bigfoot: Part 1." Aired February 1, 1976, NBC.

Crosland Jr., Alan, dir. *The Six Million Dollar Man*. Season 3, episode 18, "The Secret of Bigfoot: Part 2." Aired February 4, 1976, NBC.

Cryptid. Board Game Geek. Accessed November 26, 2022. https://boardgamegeek.com/boardgame/246784/cryptid.

"Cryptid." Grammarist.com. Accessed June 30, 2022. https://grammarist.com/usage/cryptid.

"Cryptids of North America–GLO Record of the Week for October 25, 2020." Bureau of Land Management–ArcGIS Story Maps. October 25, 2020. https://storymaps.arcgis.com/stories/ee742b9287c547d4acdfc2382213cfd3.

Dalea, Natalie. "The Strange Case of the Loveland Frog, Ohio's Amphibian Cryptid." The Portalist. July 29, 2020. https://theportalist.com/the-loveland-frog?amp=1.

Davidson, Barbara. "The American Bestiary: The Most Famous Mythical Creature of Every US State, Illustrated." CashNetUSA.com. March 20, 2019. https://www.cashnetusa.com/blog/most-famous-mythical-creature-of-every-us-state-illustrated.

Davis, Josh. "Megolodon: The Truth About the Largest Shark That Ever Lived." *Natural History Museum*. Accessed November 27, 2022. https://www.nhm.ac.uk/discover/megalodon--the-truth-about-the-largest-shark-that-ever-lived.html.

Davis, Josh. "The Siberian Unicorn Lived at The Same Time as Modern Humans." *Natural History Museum*. November 26, 2018. https://www.nhm.ac.uk/discover/news/2018/november/the-siberian-unicorn-lived-at-the-same-time-as-modern-humans.html.

Davis, Lauren. "7 Real Life Forms That People Once Believed Were Hoaxes." *Gizmodo*. March 27, 2015. https://gizmodo.com/7-real-organisms-that-people-once-believed-were-hoaxes-1694097095.

de Lazaro, Enrico. "100,000-Year-Old Fossil of Giant Vampire Bat Found in Argentina." *Sci News*. July 26, 2021. https://www.sci.news/paleontology/desmodus-draculae-fossil-09898.html.

Dear, Williams, dir. *Harry and the Hendersons*. Universal City, CA: Universal Pictures, 1987.

Debruyne, Régis, Arnaud Van Holt, Veronique Barriel, and Pascal Tassy. "Status of the So-Called African Pygmy Elephant (Loxodonta Pumilio (Noack 1906): Phylogeny of Cytochrome B and Mitochondrial Control Region Sequences." *Comptes Rendus Biologies* 326, no. 7 (2003): 687–97. https://pubmed.ncbi.nlm.nih.gov/14556388.

Demick, George, dir. Taku-He. Nashville, TN: Flickering Candle Productions, 2017.

"The Devil's Snare." FutilityCloset.com. March 6, 2011. https://www.futilitycloset.com/2011/03/06/the-devils-snare.

"Do You Know That Issie, the Japanese Loch Ness Monster, Lives in Ikeda Lake?" PeakExperienceJapan.com. September 24, 2019. https://www.peak-experience-japan.com/blog/505.

Docter, Pete, David Silverman, and Lee Unkrich, dirs. *Monsters Inc*. Emeryville, California: Pixar, 2001.

Eames, JC, R Eve, and AW Tordoff. "The Importance of Vu Quang Nature Reserve, Vietnam, for Bird Conservation, in the Context of the Annamese Lowlands Endemic Bird Area." Bird Conservation International (2001) 11:247–285. https://www.cambridge.org/core/services/aop-cambridge-core/content/view/1D722DEC09667CF4AD432A2B3E1A91F2/S0959270901000326a.pdf/the-importance-of-vu-quang-nature-reserve-vietnam-for-bird-conservation-in-the-context-of-the-annamese-lowlands-endemic-bird-area.pdf.

Eberhart, George M. *Mysterious Creatures: A Guide to Cryptozoology, Volume 2*. CA: ABC-CLIO, 2002.

Edwards, Alan. "Bear Lake Monster Gets No Respect." *Deseret News*. August 9, 2003. https://www.deseret.com/2003/8/9/19740541/bear-lake-monster-gets-no-respect.

Elkind, Daniel. "Impossible Animals: Bernard Heuvelmans and the Making of Cryptozoology." WeAretheMutants.com. October 6, 2020. https://wearethemutants.com/2020/10/06/impossible-animals-bernard-heuvelmans-and-the-making-of-cryptozoology.

Ellis, Taylor. "Stay Away from Connecticut's Most Haunted Street after Dark or You May Be Sorry." Only in Your State. August 29, 2022. https://www.onlyinyourstate.com/connecticut/velvet-street-ct.

"The Elusive Ayia Napa Sea Monster–Is It Really Out There?" *Ancient Origins*. Last updated April 24, 2019. https://www.ancient-origins .net/myths-legends-europe/ayia-napa-sea-monster-0011785.

"Extinct Teratorn (Family Teratornithidae) Fact Sheet: Summary." San Diego Zoo Wildlife Alliance Library. Accessed November 26, 2022. https://ielc.libguides.com/sdzg/factsheets/extinctteratorn.

Fairclough, Caty. "From Mermaids to Manatees: The Myth and the Reality." Smithsonian–Ocean. March 2014. https://ocean.si.edu /ocean-life/marine-mammals/mermaids-manatees-myth-and-reality.

Favreau, Jon, dir. *Elf*. New York: Guy Walks Into a Bar Productions, 2003.

Fears, Danika. "That Time Ringling Bros. Claimed It Had Real Unicorns." *New York Post*. March 2, 2017. https://nypost.com/2017/03/02/how -unicorns-became-stars-of-the-greatest-show-on-earth/amp.

"Film of 'France and the Jew' Exhibition." Experiencing History. Accessed November 10, 2022. https://perspectives.ushmm.org/item /film-of-france-and-the-jew-exhibition.

Fisher, April. "The Legend of the Northfield Pigman, with Folklorist Joseph Citro." *Burlington Free Press*. October 28, 2022. https://www .burlingtonfreepress.com/story/life/2022/10/28/northfield-pigman -joseph-citro-digs-into-the-legend-devils-washbowl-vermont /69590062007.

"Fishers." Mass Audubon. Accessed November 20, 2022. https://www .massaudubon.org/learn/nature-wildlife/mammals/fishers.

Fitzgerald, Caitlin. "The Al-Mi'Raj." CaitlinFitzgeraldArt.com. May 22, 2019. https://caitlinfitzgeraldart.com/the-al-miraj.

Fraga, Kaleena, and John Kuroski. "Meet the Yowie, the Bigfoot-Like Cryptid That's Terrified Australia for Centuries." All That's Interesting. Last updated August 14, 2022. https://allthatsinteresting.com/yowie.

Freeman, Richard. *Adventures in Cryptozoology: Hunting for Yetis, Mongolian Deathworms and Other Not-So-Mythical Monsters,* volume 1. Coral Gables, FL: Mango, 2019.

Freeman, Richard. "Have We Found Evidence of the Elusive Orang Pendek?" *The Guardian*. October 7, 2011. https://amp.theguardian .com/science/2011/oct/07/evidence-elusive-orang-pendek.

Gates, Josh, dir. *Destination Truth*. Season 4, episode 5, "Siberian Snowman." Aired October 7, 2010, SyFy.

Gates, Tucker, dir. *The X-Files*. Season 4, episode 11, "El Mundo Gira." Aired January 12, 1997.

Gavin, Karrie. "Pennsylvania Dutch History and Way of Life." Hachette Book Group. October 1, 2021. https://perma.cc/P44H-BYS5.

Geda, Curt, dir. *Scooby-Doo! Mystery Incorporated*. Season 2, episode 5, "The Hodag of Horror." Aired August 3, 2012.

Geers, Jacob. "Based on a True Story." The Culture Crush. June 4, 2019. https://www.theculturecrush.com/feature/based-on-a-true -story?format=amp.

Geller, Professor. "Man-Eating Tree." Mythology.net. Last updated March 21, 2017. https://mythology.net/mythical-creatures/man-eating -tree.

Ghai, Rajat. "Will the Indian Army's Yeti Post Boost Interest in Cryptozoology?" *DownToEarth*. April 30, 2019. https://www .downtoearth.org.in/blog/science-technology/will-the-indian-army -s-yeti-post-boost-interest-in-cryptozoology--64276.

"Giant Santa Monica Squid." Hoaxes.org. January 10, 2014. http:// hoaxes.org/weblog/comments/giant_squid.

Glover, Chloe. "Beached Giant Squid Picture That Went Viral Is Deemed a HOAX." *Mirror*. January 10, 2014. https://www.mirror.co.uk/news /weird-news/beached-giant-squid-picture-went-3008620?int_source =amp_continue_reading&int_medium=amp&int_campaign =continue_reading_button#amp-readmore-target.

"Goldencrowned Flying Fox." Batcon.org. Accessed November 12, 2022. https://www.batcon.org/article/goldencrowned-flying-fox.

Gore, Leada. "Alabama's 'Most Mythical Creature' Is One You've Probably Not Heard Of." Advance Local. March 25, 2019. https:// www.al.com/news/2019/03/alabamas-most-mythical-creature-is -one-youve-probably-not-heard-of.html?outputType=amp.

Grondahl, Paul. "Charles Hoy Fort (1874-1932): Author, Publisher and Bon Vivant Who Inspired the Fortean Society." *Times Union*. Last updated December 5, 2013. https://www.timesunion.com /albanyrural/article/Charles-Hoy-Fort-1874-1932-Author-publisher -4993518.php.

Grundhauser, Eric. "24 Extremely Local Cryptids You've Probably Never Heard Of." Atlas Obscura. March 18, 2019. https://www .atlasobscura.com/articles/great-local-cryptids.

Guarnieri, Catherine. "Twisted History: The Melonheads." *The Register Citizen*. May 23, 2010. https://www.registercitizen.com/news /article/TWISTED-HISTORY-The-Melonheads-12083951.php.

Guest, Val, dir. *The Abominable Snowman*. Burbank, CA: Warner Bros., 1957.

"Half Human, Half Bat: Van Meter Remembers a 1903 Visit from a Winged Monster." *Des Moines Register*. Last updated September 24, 2021. https://www.desmoinesregister.com/story/news/2015/07/01 /van-meter-remembers-1903-visit-from-winged-monster/29583469.

Hannan, Peter, dir. *CatDog*. Season 3, episode 2, "CatDog and the Great Parent Mystery." Aired November 25, 2000.

Harding, Luke. "'Monkey Man' Causes Panic Across Delhi." *The Guardian*. May 17, 2001. https://amp.theguardian.com/world/2001 /may/18/lukeharding.

"Hellbender." National Wildlife Federation. Accessed November 27, 2022. https://www.nwf.org/Educational-Resources/Wildlife-Guide /Amphibians/Hellbender.

Hess, Joni. "Is There Really A Honey Island Swamp Monster, Louisiana's Bigfoot? Curious Louisiana Answers." NOLA.com. Last updated July 10, 2022. https://www.nola.com/curious_louisiana/article _c3ff7ad8-f7da-11ec-ad38-cb074e0fc868.html.

Heussner, Ki Mae. "A Monster Discovery? It Was Just a Costume." *ABC News*. February 10, 2009. https://abcnews.go.com/amp/Technology /AheadoftheCurve/story?id=5610329&page=1.

Heuvelmans, Bernard. *On the Track of Unknown Animals (Abridged)*. London: Granada Publishing, 1965. https://archive.org/details /heuvelmans-bernard-on-the-track-of-unknown-animals-abridged -1970-kk-beb/page/132/mode/2up?q=Pygmy+elephant.

"The Hidebehind." AstonishingLegends.com. July 26, 2018. https:// www.astonishinglegends.com/astonishing-legends/2018/7/26/the -hidebehind.

Higashitani, Kohei. "Japan's 'Bigfoot' Still Influences Hiroshima Town after 50 years." *The Asahi Simbun*. August 13, 2020. https://www .asahi.com/sp/ajw/articles/13584940.

Holloway, April. "The Menehune of Hawaii–Ancient Race or Fictional Fairytale." AncientOrigins.net. June 11, 2014. https://www.ancient-origins.net/myths-legends/menehune-hawaii-ancient-race-or-fictional-fairytale-001741.

"Hominid." Merriam-Webster. Accessed November 10, 2022. https://www.merriam-webster.com/dictionary/hominid.

"Honey Island Swamp Monster." Mississippi Gulf Coast National Heritage Area. Accessed October 31, 2022. https://msgulfcoastheritage.ms.gov/historic/sites/honey-island-swamp-monster.

Hook, Chris. "What Is a Yowie? In Search of Australia's Own Bigfoot Legend." *7News AU*. Last updated February 27, 2022. https://7news.com.au/news/australia/what-is-a-yowie-in-search-of-australias-own-bigfoot-legend--c-5776257.amp.

Houck Jr., Joy N., dir. *Creature from Black Lake*. New Orleans: Howco International, 1976.

"The Houston Gargoyle: A Strange Sighting at NASA's Space Center." AnomAlien.com. October 17, 2018. https://anomalien.com/the-houston-gargoyle-a-strange-sighting-at-nasas-space-center.

"How the 'Spirit of the Lake' Evolved into the Smiling Ogopogo Mascot." Infotel.ca. July 11, 2015. https://infotel.ca/newsitem/how-the-spirit-of-the-lake-evolved-into-the-smiling-ogopogo-mascot/it21126.

Howard, Georgina. "Basajaun–Basque Mythology or History?" PyreneanExperience.com. February 26, 2015. https://www.pyreneanexperience.com/basajaun-and-basque-mythology.

"Hubei Shennongjia." UNESCO World Heritage Convention. Accessed October 22, 2022. https://whc.unesco.org/en/list/1509.

Hugo, Kristin. "When Unicorns Walked the Earth." *Ripley's*. December 4, 2019. https://www.ripleys.com/weird-news/unicorn-goats.

Hussein, Sara. "Modern Phoenix: The Bird Brought Back from Extinction in Japan." Phys.org. June 21, 2022. https://phys.org/news/2022-06-modern-phoenix-bird-brought-extinction.amp.

"If Bigfoot Isn't in Georgia, Where Is He?" *NPR*. August 23, 2008. https://www.npr.org/2008/08/23/93900165/if-bigfoot-isnt-in-georgia-where-is-he.

"In Search of the Dark Watchers." DarkWatchersBook.com. Accessed November 16, 2022. http://www.darkwatchersbook.com.

"In The Footsteps of The Yeti: The Hunt For Mande Barung." *The Independent*. August 11, 2008. https://www.independent.co.uk /news/world/asia/in-the-footsteps-of-the-yeti-the-hunt-for-mande -burung-890306.html.

"Is Amomongo the 'Bigfoot' Version of the Philippines?" *SunStar*. October 31, 2020. https://www.sunstar.com.ph/ampArticle /1875300.

"Jack Pearl." *LA Times*. Accessed November 20, 2022. https://projects .latimes.com/hollywood/star-walk/jack-pearl/index.html.

Janos, Adam. "What Realy Happened at Roswell?" *History*. Last Updated January 8, 2021. https://www.history.com/.amp/news/roswell-ufo -aliens-what-happened.

Janssen, Volker. "How the 'Little Green Men' Phenomenon Began on a Kentucky Farm." *History*. January 2, 2020. https://www.history.com /.amp/news/little-green-men-origins-aliens-hopkinsville-kelly.

Jen. I Live at Night podcast, Season 1, Episode 2. "Cryptids: The Alabama White Thang and Alaska's Tizheruk." September 2022. https://zencastr.com/z/boBKdEMe.

Jensen, Scott. "Creature Resembling Loch-Ness Monster Spotted in Lake Norman." Charlotte Stories. March 31, 2020. https://www .charlottestories.com/creature-resembling-loch-ness-monster -spotted-lake-norman.

Jessica. "Meet Issie, Japan's Very Own Loch Ness Monster." SoraNews24.com. September 30, 2014. https://soranews24.com /2014/09/30/meet-issie-japans-very-own-loch-ness-monster/amp.

John, Finn J.D. "Offbeat Oregon: 'Colossal Claude,' the Great Columbia Bar Sea Serpent." *The News Guard*. Last updated February 5, 2020. https://www.thenewsguard.com/community_paid/offbeat-oregon -colossal-claude-the-great-columbia-bar-sea-serpent/article_7df40f0a -4773-11ea-acf4-678991ac3ee4.html.

Johnson, Dean. "If Today's News Is Beyond Belief, Don't Believe It." *Orlando Sentinel*. April 1, 1985. https://www.orlandosentinel.com /news/os-xpm-1985-04-01-0290000216-story.html.

Johnson, Eric Michael. "A Natural History of Vampires." *Scientific American*. October 31, 2011. https://blogs.scientificamerican.com /primate-diaries/a-natural-history-of-vampires.

Johnson, W. Hilton. "Pleistocene Epoch." *Encyclopedia Britannica*. Last updated November 22, 2022. https://www.britannica.com/science /Pleistocene-Epoch.

Jones, V. L. "New Hampshire's Wood Devils." CoffeeHouseWriters.com. April 19, 2021. https://coffeehousewriters.com/new-hampshires -wood-devils.

Jovanovic, Dragana. "Vampire Threat Terrorizes Serbian Village." *ABC News*. November 18, 2012. https://abcnews.go.com/International /vampire-threat-terrorizes-serbian-village/story?id=17831327# .ULdq69Pjnop.

Kadane, Lisa. "Canada's Mysterious Lake Monster." *BBC*. March 10, 2020. https://www.bbc.com/travel/article/20200309-ogopogo-the -monster-lurking-in-okanagan-lake.

Kadane, Lisa. "The True Origin Of Sasquatch." *BBC*. July 21, 2022. https://www.bbc.com/travel/article/20220720-the-true-origin-of -sasquatch.

Kelly, Walt. *I Go Pogo*. New York: Simon and Schuster, 1952. https:// archive.org/details/igopogokell00kell/page/n6/mode/1up?view =theater.

Klimczak, Natalia. "Aspidochelone: A Giant Sea Monster of the Ancient World and an Allegorical Beast." *Ancient Origins*. Last updated January 21, 2016. https://www.ancient-origins.net/myths-legends /aspidochelone-giant-sea-monster-ancient-world-and-allegorical -beast-005210.

Krofft, Marty, Sid Krofft, and Si Rose, created by. *Sigmund and the Sea Monsters*. NBC, 1973–1975.

Kuperinsky, Amy. "The (Jersey) Devil Within: Unmasking the Prudential Center's Resident Demon." NJ.com. March 12, 2015. https://www.nj .com/entertainment/2015/03/new_jersey_devils_mascot_nj_devil _prudential_cente.html.

Lange, Jeva. "The Lord God Bird and A Growing Class of Cryptids." *The Week*. October 13, 2021. https://theweek.com/science/1005980/the -lord-god-bird-and-a-growing-class-of-cryptids?amp.

Law, Zoe. "In Japan, A Real-Life Phoenix Rises from the Ashes of Extinction." *South China Morning Post*. June 23, 2022. https://www .scmp.com/video/environment/3182805/japan-real-life-phoenix -rises-ashes-extinction.

Lawrence, Katie. "The Legend of the Mongollon Monster in Arizona May Send Chills Down Your Spine." OnlyInYourState.com. December 16, 2021. https://www.onlyinyourstate.com/arizona/mogollon -monster-az/amp.

"The Legend of Walking Sam." HorrorHub.com. June 8, 2021. https:// horrorhubmarketplace.com/legends/the-legend-of-walking-sam.

"A Legendary Sea Creature." The J. Paul Getty Museum. Accessed October 14, 2022. https://www.getty.edu/education/kids_families /do_at_home/artscoops/sea_creature.html.

"Leviathan." *Encyclopedia Britannica*, August 29, 2022. https://www .britannica.com/topic/Leviathan-Middle-Eastern-mythology.

Levs, Josh. "Bigfoot Hoax Ends in Death, Authorities Say." *CNN*. Last updated August 28, 2012. https://www.cnn.com/2012/08/28/us /montana-big-foot-accident/index.html.

Lin, Kimberly. "Cadborosaurus: Sea Serpent, Dinosaur, or Myth?" Historic Mysteries. Accessed November 8, 2022. https://www .historicmysteries.com/cadborosaurus/,

Lotzof, Kerry. "Sea Monsters and Their Inspiration: Serpents, Mermaids, the Kraken and More." *Natural History Museum*. Accessed October 25, 2022. https://www.nhm.ac.uk/discover/sea-monsters-inspiration -serpents-mermaids-the-kraken.html.

Madden, Duncan. "Fantastic Cryptids and Where to Find Them." *Forbes*. November 16, 2018. https://www.forbes.com/sites/duncanmadden /2018/11/16/fantastic-cryptids-and-where-to-find-them/?sh =45798c601d99.

"Maher, John G." History Nebraska. Accessed November 26, 2022. https://history.nebraska.gov/publications_section/maher-john-g.

"Mange." Cornell Wildlife Health Lab. Accessed August 16, 2022. https://cwhl.vet.cornell.edu/disease/mange.

Manners, Kim, dir, *The X-Files*. Season 3, episode 22, "Quagmire." Aired May 3, 1996.

"Mapinguari: Beast of South America." Majestic Blends. Accessed November 10, 2022. https://majesticblends.com/blogs/coffee /mapinguari-beast-of-south-america.

Martins, Ralph. "New Species of See-Through Frog Found, Looks Like Kermit." *National Geographic*. April 21, 2015. https://www .hindustantimes.com/science/zsi-scientists-discover-new-macaque -species-in-arunachal-pradesh-101653736625665.html.

McCarthy, Erin. "22 Creepy Cryptids from Around the World." MentalFloss. September 27, 2021. https://www.mentalfloss.com /article/649386/cryptids-around-the-world.

McCulloch, Christopher, dir. *Venture Bros.* Season 1, Episode 1, "Dia de los Dangerous." Aired August 7, 2004, Cartoon Network.

McCulloch, Christopher, dir. *Venture Bros.* Season 1, Episode 3, "Home Insecurity." Aired August 21, 2004, Cartoon Network.

McConnell, Kelsey Christine. "The Enfield Monster: Alien, Cryptid, or Incident of Mass Hysteria?" TheLineup.com. June 21, 2022. https:// the-line-up.com/the-enfield-monster?amp=1.

McGannon D. C. and C. Michael McGannon. "5 Legendary Monsters of North American Folklore." Folklore Thursday. August 24, 2017. https://folklorethursday.com/halloween/legendary-monsters-north -american-folklore/#_edn14.

McGough, Tom, dir. *Alien Autopsy: (Fact or Fiction?).* NY: FOX, 1995. https://www.imdb.com/title/tt0163521.

Meier, Allison. "How a Fake Monster Crept into Our Museums." *Hyperallergic.* January 15, 2018. https://hyperallergic.com/421405 /how-a-fake-monster-creeped-into-our-museums.

Mendelson, Joe. "Are Jackalopes Real?" Zoo Atlanta. November 8, 2021. https://zooatlanta.org/are-jackalopes-real.

Monahan, Richard, dir. "Finding Bigfoot." Silver Springs, MD: Animal Planet, 2011.

Monk, Matthew. "Dive into the Terrifying Legend of the Lake Worth Monster." Texas Hill Country. July 1, 2018. https://texashillcountry .com/legend-of-lake-worth-monster.

"A Monster's Expedition." Nintendo. Accessed October 26, 2022. https://www.nintendo.com/store/products/a-monsters-expedition -switch.

Monsterquest. Season 4, Episode 9. "America's Werewolf." Aired March 24, 2010. History Channel.

Murphy, Elias. "Column: The Tennessee Wildman." East Tennessean Online. September 21, 2022. https://easttennessean.com/2022/09 /21/column-the-tennessee-wildman.

Murphy, Kevin, dir. *Mystery Science Theater 3000.* Season 11, episode 6, "Boggy Creek II: And the Legend Continues." Aired May 9. 1999.

"The Mythic Child-Stealing Thunderbirds of Illinois." *Atlas Obscura*. August 5, 2015. https://www.atlasobscura.com/articles/the-mythic -child-stealing-thunderbirds-of-illinois.

"Nahanni Butte." SpectacularNorthwestTerritories.com. Accessed November 8, 2022. https://spectacularnwt.com/destinations /dehcho/nahanni-butte.

Naish, Darren. "A Baby Sea-Serpent No More: Reinterpreting Hagelund's Juvenile Cadborosaurus." *Scientific American*. September 26, 2011. https://blogs.scientificamerican.com/tetrapod-zoology/baby-sea -serpent-no-more.

Naish, Darren. "Is Cryptozoology Good or Bad for Science?" *Scientific American*. September 17, 2014. https://blogs.scientificamerican.com /tetrapod-zoology/is-cryptozoology-good-or-bad-for-science.

Napolitano, Joe, dir. *The X-Files*. Season 1, episode 5, "The Jersey Devil." Aired October 8, 1993.

"Native Animals." New Zealand Department of Conservation. Accessed November 12, 2022. https://www.doc.govt.nz/nature/native -animals.

"A New Underground Monster." *Nature* 17 (1878): 325-326. https:// books.google.co.uk/books?id=RIxFAAAAYAAJ&vq=Minhoc %C3%A3o%20worm&dq=Minhoc%C3%A3o%20worm&pg =PA325#v=snippet&q=Minhoc%C3%A3o%20worm&f=false.

Nickell, Joe. "Gloucester Sea-Serpent Mystery: Solved after Two Centuries." *Skeptical Inquirer* 43, no. 5. (2019). https:// skepticalinquirer.org/2019/09/gloucester-sea-serpent-mystery -solved-after-two-centuries.

Nickell, Joe. "Siege of the 'Little Green Men': The 1955 Kelly, Kentucky, Incident." *Skeptical Inquirer*. November/December 2006, Volume 30, No. 6. https://skepticalinquirer.org/2006/11/siege-of-little-green -men-the-1955-kelly-kentucky-incident.

Nickell, Joe. "Steller's Sea Ape: Identifying an Eighteenth-Century Cryptid." *Skeptical Inquirer*. April 24, 2017. https://skepticalinquirer .org/newsletter/stellers-sea-ape-identifying-an-eighteenth-century -cryptid.

Nickell, Joe. "Zanzibar's Popobawa Demon Still Attacking Skeptics." CenterforInquiry.org. March 15, 2018. https://centerforinquiry .org/blog/zanzibars_popobawa_demon_still_attacking_skeptics.

"Night of the Tommyknockers Western Horror Film!" Indiegogo. Accessed December 26, 2022. https://www.indiegogo.com/projects /night-of-the-tommyknockers-western-horror-film#.

"Nittaewo–The Dagger Clawed Pygmies of Sri Lanka." Srilanka.Travel. Accessed November 30, 2022. https://srilanka.travel/nittaewo-in -srilanka.

Noebes, Magalie. "Move Over Bigfoot, the Slide-Rock Bolter Is Colorado's Rarest Cryptid." Our Community Now. August 24, 2022. https://ourcommunitynow.com/local-culture/move-over-bigfoot-the -slide-rock-bolter-is-colorados-rarest-cryptid.

Norton, Bill, dir. "Baby: Secret of the Lost Legend." Burbank, CA: Touchstone Films, 1985.

O'Mahony, Mike. *Deadly Detour: The Goat Man Murders*. Somerset, England: Maniac Films, 2011.

Ocker, J.W. "Beware the Thunderbird, Badass Cryptid of the Skies." *Atlas Obscura*. October 26, 2022. https://www.atlasobscura.com /articles/thunderbird-cryptid-ocker.amp.

Oda, Eiichirô, created by. *One Piece*. Toei Animation, 1999.

Offutt, Jason. "Exploring American Monsters: Connecticut." Mysterious Universe. April 13, 2015. https://mysteriousuniverse.org/2015/04 /exploring-american-monsters-Connecticut.

Offutt, Jason. "Exploring American Monsters: Nebraska." Mysterious Universe. December 22, 2015. https://mysteriousuniverse.org/2015 /12/exploring-american-monsters-Nebraska.

Offutt, Jason. "Exploring American Monsters: North Carolina." Mysterious Universe. April 29, 2016. https://mysteriousuniverse.org /2016/04/exploring-american-monsters-north-carolina.

"Orang Pendek." Wild Sumatra. Accessed November 1, 2022. https:// www.wildsumatra.com/orang-pendek.

Osborne, Lindi. "Meet Bessie, the Loch Ness Monster of Lake Erie." Great Lakes Guide. October 16, 2020. https://greatlakes.guide/ideas /meet-bessie-the-loch-ness-monsters-canadian-cousin-livin.

"Our Story." Yeti.com. Accessed November 11, 2022. https://stories.yeti .com/story/our-story?_ga=2.85366105.1978982506.1668242452 -948384867.1668242452&_gac=1.174924182.1668242452 .EAIaIQobChMI0NjNsZ-o-wIVTtyGCh3AYgsJEAAYASAAEgLH4fD _BwE.

Owens, Sara. "The Big Grey Man." NationalParanormalSociety.com. March 1, 2022. http://national-paranormal-society.org/am-fear -liath-mor.

"Pareidolia." Merriam-Webster. Accessed October 11, 2022. https:// www.merriam-webster.com/dictionary/pareidolia.

Parquette, Archer. "The Legend of the Beast of Bray Road." *Milwaukee Magazine*. October 30, 2020. https://www.milwaukeemag.com /the-legend-of-the-beast-of-bray-road.

"Pecos Bill." *Encyclopedia Britannica*. February 20, 2014. https://www .britannica.com/topic/Pecos-Bill.

Pellington, Mark, dir. *The Mothman Prophecies*. Beverly Hills, CA: Lakeshore Entertainment, 2002.

Pierce, Charles B., dir. *Boggy Creek II: And the Legend Continues*. New Orleans: Howco International Pictures, 1984.

Pierce, Charles B., dir. *The Legend of Boggy Creek*. Arkansas: Pierce -Ledwell Productions, 1972.

"Piltdown Man." Natural History Museum. Accessed July 22, 2022. https://www.nhm.ac.uk/our-science/departments-and-staff/library -and-archives/collections/piltdown-man.html.

"The Place–Fact or Fiction: Momo, the Missouri Monster." KY3.com. March 10, 2022. https://www.ky3.com/2022/03/10/place-fact-or -fiction-momo-missouri-monster/?outputType=amp.

The Police. 1983. "Synchronicity II." Track #6 on *Synchronicity*. A&M Records.

Polly, P. David. "Diprotodon." *Encyclopedia Britannica*. December 15, 2017. https://www.britannica.com/animal/Diprotodon.

Price, Mark. "Was It a Chupacabra? NC Biologists Try to Identify Spooky Creature Seen in the Dark." *The Charlotte Observer*. Last updated April 8, 2018. https://amp.charlotteobserver.com/news/local /article209109824.html.

"Project BLUE BOOK–Unidentified Flying Objects." National Archives. Accessed July 22, 2022. https://www.archives.gov/research/military /air-force/ufos.

Prothero, Donald R., and Daniel Loxton. *Abominable Science!: Origins of the Yeti, Nessie, and Other Famous Cryptids*. New York: Columbia University Press, 2013.

"Radar/CatDog." TV Tropes. Accessed November 30, 2022. https:// tvtropes.org/pmwiki/pmwiki.php/Radar/CatDog.

Radford, Benjamin. "Mistaken Memories of Vampires: Pseudohistories of the Chupacabra." *Skeptical Inquirer* 40, no. 1 (2016). https://skepticalinquirer.org/wp-content/uploads/sites/29/2016/01/SI-JF-16-50.pdf.

Radford, Benjamin. "The Monkey Man Panic: 20 Years Later." *Skeptical Inquirer*. May 21, 2021. https://skepticalinquirer.org/exclusive/the-monkey-man-panic-20-years-later.

Rafferty, J. P. "Gigantopithecus." *Encyclopedia Britannica*. September 15, 2022. https://www.britannica.com/animal/Gigantopithecus.

Rafferty, Rachel. "The Myths and Legends of Ireland's Hound of Deep, The Dobhar Chu." IrishCentral. May 30, 2021. https://www.irishcentral.com/roots/irelands-hound-dobhar-chu.amp.

"The Rake." Dictionary.com. Accessed November 27, 2022. https://www.dictionary.com/e/fictional-characters/the-rake.

"Recap/The Simpsons S1 E7 'The Call of the Simpsons.'" TVTropes.org. Accessed November 11, 2022. https://tvtropes.org/pmwiki/pmwiki.php/Recap/TheSimpsonsS1E7TheCallOfTheSimpsons.

Redfern, Nick. "Boggy Creek Casebook: A New Book Reviewed." Mysterious Universe. November 26, 2020. https://mysteriousuniverse.org/2020/11/boggy-creek-casebook-a-new-book-reviewed.

Regal, Brian. "Yeti Hunters Must Be More Scientific." *The Guardian*. October 12, 2011. https://amp.theguardian.com/commentisfree/2011/oct/12/yeti-hunters-scientific-russian-cryptozoologists.

"Resolution Declaring a Sasquatch/Bigfoot Sanctuary." City of Norton, Virginia. October 21, 2014. http://www.nortonva.gov/DocumentCenter/View/1956/Woodbooger-Resolution?bidId=.

Rettner, Rachael. "3 Human Chimeras That Already Exist." *Scientific American*. August 8, 2016. https://www.scientificamerican.com/article/3-human-chimeras-that-already-exist.

Robinson, Charles T. "Vampire Mercy Brown | When Rhode Island Was 'The Vampire Capital of America.'" NewEngland.com. October 4, 2022. https://newengland.com/today/living/new-england-history/vampire-mercy-brown-rhode-island.

Rodgers, Rene. "Favorite Festivals in Tennessee and Virginia." BirthplaceofCountryMusic.org. September 7, 2021. https://birthplaceofcountrymusic.org/tag/woodbooger.

Rogers, K. "Chimera." *Encyclopedia Britannica*. December 3, 2018. https://www.britannica.com/science/chimera-genetics.

Roper, Clyde, Dr. "Giant Squid *Architeuthis dux*." *Smithsonian*. April 2018. https://ocean.si.edu/ocean-life/invertebrates/giant-squid.

Rossen, Jake. "E.T. or B.S.? When Fox Aired Its Famous 'Alien Autopsy' in 1995." Mental Floss. October 6, 2022. https://www.mentalfloss .com/posts/fox-1995-alien-autopsy-hoax.

Salvador, Rodrigo Brincalepe. "The Real-Life Origins of The Legendary Kraken." The Conversation. December 30, 2015. https:// theconversation.com/amp/the-real-life-origins-of-the-legendary -kraken-52058.

Salvador, Rodrigo B., and Barbara M. Tomotani. "The Kraken: When Myth Encounters Science." *História, Ciências, Saúde–Manguinhos* 21, no. 3 (2014): 971–994. https://www.scielo.br/j /hcsm/a/3f7pGvQSBQNC4kkC8MXsbQQ/?format=pdf&lang=en.

Sanders, Savannah. "Everything You Need to Know about Expedition Everest." TouringPlans.com. September 8, 2019. https://touringplans .com/blog/everything-you-need-to-know-about-expedition-everest.

"Saola." World Wildlife Fund. Accessed July 17, 2022. https://www .worldwildlife.org/species/saola.

Sarkar, Donna. "The Legend of the Wolpertinger, the Horned Rabbit Said to Roam the Bavarian Alps." All That's Interesting. November 9, 2022. https://allthatsinteresting.com/wolpertinger.

"Sasquatch." *Marvel*. Accessed November 19, 2022. https://www .marvel.com/characters/sasquatch-walter-langkowski.

"Sasquatch (Walter Langkowski): Comics." *Marvel*. Accessed November 19, 2022. https://www.marvel.com/comics/characters/1009560 /sasquatch_walter_langkowski?byZone=marvel_site_zone&offset =0&byType=character&dateStart=&dateEnd=&orderBy=release _date+desc&formatType=issue,digitalcomic,collection&byId =1009560&limit=8&count=10&totalcount=93.

"Sava Savanovic: Most Famous Serbian Vampire." MeettheSlavs.com. Last updated May 14, 2022. https://meettheslavs.com/sava -savanovic.

"Scape Ore Swamp." Roadtrippers.com. Accessed November 27, 2022. https://maps.roadtrippers.com/us/bishopville-sc/nature/scape-ore -swamp.

Schneck, Marcus. "Pennsylvania's Squonk Is 'The Homeliest Animal in The World': Monsters of Pennsylvania." PennLive.com. Last updated

June 26, 2015. https://www.pennlive.com/wildaboutpa/2015/06
/pennsylvanias_squonk_ends_the.html.

Schulte, David, dir. *Monstrum*. Season 4, episode 6, "Mapinguari:
Fearsome Beast and Protector of the Amazon." Aired June 2, 2022,
PBS. https://www.pbs.org/video/mapinguari-fearsome-beast-and
-protector-of-the-amazon-xnse9d.

Scott, Leigh, dir. *The Beast of Bray Road*. Burbank, CA: The Asylum,
2005.

"Seals, Sea Lions and Walruses." The Marine Mammal Center. Accessed
November 13, 2022. https://www.marinemammalcenter.org/animal
-care/learn-about-marine-mammals/pinnipeds.

Seariac, Hanna. "The Legendary Tale of Brigham Young and the Bear
Lake Monster(s)." *Deseret News*. May 21, 2022. https://www.deseret
.com/utah/2022/5/21/23130943/bear-lake-monster-tale-origins
-brigham-young-utah-idaho?_amp=true.

"Seeing a Cephalopod in Ancient Bones." *NPR*. October 14, 2011.
https://www.npr.org/2011/10/14/141356526/seeing-a-cephalopod
-in-ancient-bones.

"Selbyville Swamp Monster: Fact or Fiction..." Shorebread.com. May
27, 2014. https://shorebread.com/2014/05/27/selbyville-swamp
-monster-fact-or-fiction.

"Seven Species That Used to Be Cryptids." Indiana University
Bloomington. December 12, 2020. https://blogs.iu.edu/sciu/2020
/12/12/seven-cryptids-species.

"Seven Cryptids Way Cooler Than Bigfoot." All That's Interesting.
Last updated November 16, 2021. https://allthatsinteresting.com
/%20cryptids.

"Sharlie the Payette Lake Monster." VisitMcCall.org. Accessed November
20, 2022. https://visitmccall.org/sharlie-payette-lake-monster.

Shermer, Michael. "The Sensed-Presence Effect." *Scientific American*.
April 1, 2010. https://www.scientificamerican.com/article/the
-sensed-presence-effect.

Shovelin, Emilia. "We Were Confronted by A Bigfoot-Like 'Yowie'
Apeman on Our Way Home from Work." *New York Post*. December
14, 2021. https://nypost.com/2021/12/14/we-were-confronted-by
-a-bigfoot-like-yowie-apeman/amp.

Shuker, Karl. "The Curious Case of Rothschild's Lost Tusk and
the Non-Existent Elephant Pig—An Enduring Cryptozoological

Conundrum from Africa." *Shuker Nature* (blog). July 3, 2014. http://
karlshuker.blogspot.com/2014/07/the-curious-case-of-rothschilds
-lost.html?m=1.

Shuker, Karl. 2020. "The 'Other' Orang Pendek," *Fortean Times* No. 398
(November). ZINIO Unlimited.

"Siberian Unicorn' Discovery Shocks Scientists." All That's Interesting.
Last updated November 27, 2018. https://allthatsinteresting.com
/siberian-unicorn-elasmotherium-sibiricum.

Siddiqui, Dr. Raheal Ahmad. "In Search of an Elusive Creature." *The
International News*. February 16, 2014. https://www.thenews.com.pk
/amp/555751-search-elusive-creature.

Sieczkowski, Cavan. "Save Savanovic, Vampire, May Be on the Loose
in Serbia, Council Says in Public Health Warning." *HuffPost*. Last
updated December 1, 2012. https://www.huffpost.com/entry/sava
-savanovic-vampire-on-the-loose-serbia_n_2211364/amp.

Sims, Andrew. "The New 'Fantastic Beasts' Book Is Out: Here's What J.
K. Rowling Adds to Canon." Hypable.com. March 14, 2017. https://
www.hypable.com/new-fantastic-beasts-book-updates/amp.

"Skunk Ape Research Headquarters–Ochopee, Florida." Atlas Obscura.
Accessed November 10, 2022. https://www.atlasobscura.com/places
/skunk-ape-research-headquarters.

Su, Michael, dir. *Night of the Tommyknockers*. Las Vegas: Mahal Empire,
2022.Wilder, W. Lee, dir. *The Snow Creature*. Los Angeles, CA: Planet
Filmplays Ltd., 1954.

"Society for the Investigation of the Unexplained (SITU)." Encyclopedia.
com. Accessed November 11, 2022. https://www.encyclopedia.com
/science/encyclopedias-almanacs-transcripts-and-maps/society
-investigation-unexplained-situ.

"Soviet Scientist Believes 'Snowmen' Are Neanderthal Survivors." *New
York Times*. February 18, 1964. https://www.nytimes.com/1964/02
/18/archives/soviet-scientist-believes-snowmen-are-neanderthal
-survivors.html

Stienstra, Tom. "Tracking the legendary Ghost Deer of Northern
California." *SFGATE*. November 9. 2003. https://www.sfgate.com
/green/article/Tracking-the-legendary-Ghost-Deer-of-Northern
-2549732.php.

"A Summary of Tennyson's Apocalyptic Poem." InterestingLiterature.
com.

Accessed November 8, 2022. https://interestingliterature.com/2016 /09/a-short-analysis-of-tennysons-the-kraken/amp.

"Superfund Site: West Virginia Ordinance (US ARMY) Point Pleasant, WV." EPA. Accessed October 29, 2022. https://cumulis.epa.gov /supercpad/cursites/csitinfo.cfm?id=0303066.

Swancer, Brent. "The Mysterious Case of the Vampire Vine of Nicaragua." Mysterious Universe. June 1, 2022. https:// mysteriousuniverse.org/2022/05/The-Mysterious-Case-of-the -Vampire-Vine-of-Nicaragua.

Swancer, Brent. "The Mysterious Dark Watchers of California." Mysterious Universe. July 3, 2018. https://mysteriousuniverse.org /2018/07/the-mysterious-dark-watchers-of-california.

Swancer, Brent. "Strange Beasts of Japan's Far North." Mysterious Universe. June 10, 2014. https://mysteriousuniverse.org/2014/06 /strange-beasts-of-japans-far-north.

Sword, JD. "Not Deer, or a Deer?" *Skeptical Inquirer*. September 10, 2021. https://skepticalinquirer.org/exclusive/not-deer-or-a-deer.

Tabler, Dave. "It's the Snallygaster." AppalachianHistory.net. November 5, 2018. https://www.appalachianhistory.net/2018/11 /its-snallygaster.html.

Tabler, Dave. "The Story of the Wampus Cat." AppalachianHistory.net. October 13, 2017. https://www.appalachianhistory.net/2017/10 /story-of-wampus-cat.html.

"Taku-He." Werewoofs.com. Accessed November 27, 2022. https:// www.werewoofs.com/monster-stories/taku-he.

"Tales of a Prehistoric Sea Monster Passed Down for Generations!" DiscoverDarien.com. Accessed November 19, 2022. https:// discoverdarien.com/our-sea-monster.

"Terror, Tourism and Odd Beliefs." *The Economist*. December 11, 2003. https://www.economist.com/middle-east-and-africa/2003/12/11 /terror-tourism-and-odd-beliefs.

"Thunderbird." *Ford*. Accessed November 8, 2022. https://corporate .ford.com/articles/history/thunderbird.html.

Thuras, Dylan. "Nepenthes Rajah: The King of the Pitcher Plants." *Atlas Obscura*. Accessed October 16, 2022. https://www.atlasobscura.com /places/nepenthes-rajah-the-king-of-the-pitcher-plants.

Tillman, Kirsten. "Ya-Te-Veo the Man Eating Tree." NationalParanormalSociety.org. January 2, 2022. http://national -paranormal-society.org/ya-te-veo-man-eating-tree.

"TNT Area–Point Pleasant, West Virginia." Atlas Obscura. Accessed October 29, 2022. https://www.atlasobscura.com/places/tnt-area.

"To Be Sherpa Is an Ethnic Heritage, Not a Profession." Adventure Access. April 13, 2021. https://adventure-access.com/sherpa-ethnic -heritage-not-profession.

Tolkien, JRR. *Tales from the Perilous Realm*. New York: Mariner Books, 2012.

Underhill, David. "10 Mystery Monster Finds with Perfectly Rational Explanations." Listverse.com. November 30, 2014. https://listverse .com/2014/11/30/10-mystery-monster-finds-with-perfectly-rational -explanation.

"Understanding Aboriginal Dreamings." Artlandish. Accessed December 26, 2022. https://www.aboriginal-art-australia.com/aboriginal-art -library/understanding-aboriginal-dreaming-and-the-dreamtime.

"The Unicorn Rests in a Garden (from the Unicorn Tapestries) 1495–1505." *MET Museum*. Accessed November 9, 2011. https:// www.metmuseum.org/art/collection/search/467642.

Vaughan, Bridget. "Mysteries, Oddities, and Everything Strange: Ya-Te-Veo." The Patriot Press. June 7, 2022. https://fthspatpress.com /24774/news/mysteries-oddities-and-everything-strange-ya-te-veo.

"Venus Flytrap." National Wildlife Federation. Accessed October 16, 2022. https://www.nwf.org/Educational-Resources/Wildlife-Guide /Plants-and-Fungi/Venus-Flytrap.

"Visit the Monster Museum." Visit Braxton. Accessed July 22, 2022. https://braxtonwv.org/the-flatwoods-monster/visit-the-museum.

"Was the Ahuizotl an Aztec Mythical Creature of a Real Fisherman's Foe?" *Ancient Origins*. Last updated April 22, 2019. https://www .ancient-origins.net/myths-legends-americas/ahuizotl-aztec-mythical -creature-or-real-fisherman-s-foe-009941.

Weisberg, Tim. "'Dover Demon' Still Mystifies Massachusetts 45 Years Later." WBSM.com. April 20, 2022. https://wbsm.com/dover-demon -massachusetts-45-years-later.

Weiser, Kathy. "Jackalopes of Wyoming–Myth or Reality?" LegendsofAmerica.com. Last updated October 2019. https://www .legendsofamerica.com/wy-jackalope.

Weiser, Kathy. "The Muscogee (Creek) Nation." LegendsofAmerica.com. March 2020. https://www.legendsofamerica.com/na-creek.

Weiser-Alexander, Kathy. "Tommyknockers of the Western Mines." LegendsofAmerica.com. Last updated November 2021. https://www.legendsofamerica.com/gh-tommyknockers.

Welch, Craig. "Mysterious New Whale Species Discovered in Alaska." *National Geographic*. July 26, 2016. https://www.nationalgeographic.com/animals/article/new-whale-species.

Wenzl, Roy. "In 1952, the Flatwoods Monster Terrified 6 Kids, a Mom, a Dog—and the Nation." *History*. Last updated January 10, 2020. https://www.history.com/.amp/news/flatwoods-monster-west-virginia.

"West Virginia Week in History–Gray Barker." *Register-Herald*. April 27, 2022. https://www.register-herald.com/news/life/west-virginia-week-in-history---gray-barker/article_749daeb2-c592-11ec-870c-ff7fad6a0db3.html.

"Western Animation/Beany and Cecil." TV Tropes. Accessed December 26, 2022. https://tvtropes.org/pmwiki/pmwiki.php/WesternAnimation/BeanyAndCecil.

"The Whale." OldEnglishPoetryProject.com. Accessed October 14, 2022. https://oldenglishpoetry.camden.rutgers.edu/the-whale.

"What is Superfund?" EPA.gov. Accessed October 29, 2022. https://www.epa.gov/superfund/what-superfund.

"What Is the Wendigo? Meet The Cannibalistic Cryptid of Your Nightmares." All That's Interesting. Last updated August 17, 2022. https://allthatsinteresting.com/wendigo.

"Who's a Good Boy? Not the Michigan Dogman." *NPR*. October 30, 2019. https://www.michiganradio.org/offbeat/2019-10-30/whos-a-good-boy-not-the-michigan-dogman?_amp=true.

Wick, Jessica. "The Cadborosaurus Is a Mysterious Sea Creature That Has Been Spotted in Washington." OnlyInYourState.com. November 22, 2020. https://www.onlyinyourstate.com/washington/the-cadborosaurus-in-wa/amp.

Wilder, Billy, dir. *The Private Life of Sherlock Holmes*. Los Angeles, CA: United Artists, 1970.

Wiley, Ethan, dir. *Journey of the Forbidden Valley*. Los Angeles, CA: Wiseacre Films, 2017.

Williams, Janice. "What's the Difference Between Yeti, Sasquatch and Bigfoot? Indian Army Claims It Found Mystery Snowman's Footprints." *Newsweek*. April 30, 2019. https://www.newsweek.com/yeti-sasquatch-bigfoot-creature-myth-1409689.

Williams, Matt. "Cottingley Fairies: The Photo Hoax That Fooled Kodak and Arthur Conan Doyle." PetaPixel. November 8, 2021. https://petapixel.com/2021/11/08/cottingley-fairies-the-photo-hoax-that-fooled-kodak-and-arthur-conan-doyle.

Willson, J. D. "Mud Snake (Farancia abacura)." Savannah River Ecology Laboratory–University of Georgia. Accessed November 27, 2022. https://srelherp.uga.edu/snakes/faraba.htm.

Wolfe, Paul. "Over a Century Ago Newspapers Reported Sightings of a Specter Moose in Maine." Q106.5.FM. Last updated October 19, 2022. https://q1065.fm/mysterious-maine-maines-specter-moose.

"Woodbooger Sanctuary." NortonVirginia.gov. Accessed November 11, 2022. https://www.nortonva.gov/455/Woodbooger-Sanctuary.

Wright, Andy. "Maryland's Goatman Is Half Man, Half Goat, and Out for Blood." Modern Farmer. September 16, 2013. https://modernfarmer.com/2013/09/marylands-goatman-half-man-half-goat-blood.

Wright, Andy. "Move Over Bigfoot, Here Comes Sheepsquatch." Modern Farmer. December 12, 2013. https://modernfarmer.com/2013/12/move-bigfoot-comes-sheepsquatch.

"zoology." Online Etymology Dictionary. Accessed July 17, 2022. https://www.etymonline.com/word/zoology.

"ZSI Scientists Discover New Macaque Species in Arunachal Pradesh." *Hindustan Times*. May 28, 2022. https://www.hindustantimes.com/science/zsi-scientists-discover-new-macaque-species-in-arunachal-pradesh-101653736625665.html.

ACKNOWLEDGMENTS

I'd like to thank my family, friends, and all of my teachers for encouraging this whole writing thing all these years.

Huge thanks to the crew at Ulysses Press, including Casie Vogel, Shelona Belfon, Paulina Maurovich, Scott Calamar, Claire Chun, Elke Barter, Winnie Liu, and anyone else who worked behind the scenes to make this book possible.

A special thanks to our nephew Chance for alerting me to the Not Deer cryptid. And a thousand thanks to the cryptozoologists, cryptozoology enthusiasts, folklorists, storytellers, and everyday folk who keep this topic alive!

ABOUT THE AUTHOR

Bernadette "Berni" Johnson began her career at age six when she crayoned a book about her mom that received a rave review from its lone reader. In her youth, she devoured the entire sci-fi section of the local library and dabbled in computer programming (and gaming) on an Atari 1200, leading to an IT career in adulthood.

She also kept one foot in humanities and literature, earned a couple of English degrees, and continued to write. Her works include over fifty technology articles for HowStuffWorks.com; *The Big Book of Spy Trivia* and *The Big Book of Horse Trivia for Kids* from Ulysses Press; and several short stories published here and there, as well as books and stories soon to come out.

When she's not watching movies and TV or fiddling with a computer, she studies history, science, and other fun stuff, reads and writes fiction and nonfiction, and does the bidding of her terrier. You can read Berni's blog and find links to her writing at bernijohnson.com.